Original Dedication

, TO THE

GREAT-GRANDCHILDREN, GRAND-NEPHEWS, AND GRAND-NIECES

OF EDWARD, 13TH EARL OF DERBY,

THIS BOOK OF DRAWINGS AND VERSES

(The greater part of which were originally made and composed for their parents,)

Is Dedicated by the Author

EDWARD LEAR.

London, 1862.

CONTENTS

CONTENTS

THE COMPLETE NONSENSE
BOOK

THE COMPLETE NON-SENSE BOOK

BY
EDWARD LEAR

Containing all the Original Pictures and Verses, together with New Material

Edited by
LADY STRACHEY
OF SUTTON COURT

Introduction by
THE EARL OF CROMER
G. C. B., G. C. M. G., K. C. S. I.

NEW YORK
DUFFIELD & COMPANY
1921

CONTENTS

CONTENTS

CONTENTS

CONTENTS

CONTENTS

[xi]

CONTENTS

CONTENTS

[xiii]

CONTENTS

CONTENTS

CONTENTS

THE COMPLETE NONSENSE
BOOK

PREFACE

By Lord Cromer

Perhaps the best monument to the memory of Edward Lear is to be found in the merry laughter which his works and drawings have excited amongst children whom he loved so well. He lives, and will continue to live, in the minds of the public as one of the great classical authors of nonsense. It is said that Dickens was wont to peruse carefully the records of births, deaths and marriages, in order to find names suitable to the characters in his novels. That he was singularly successful in the assortment of his names cannot be doubted. Although it would perhaps be difficult to assign any good reason for our opinion, we all feel that the character of the immortal Winkle could not, with any degree of onomatopœic propriety, have been assigned to a man who spoke and conducted himself like Tupman, and that Mr. and Mrs. Murdstone would have behaved quite differently if their names had been Trotwood. Who, again—to put some extreme cases—would suggest that the names of Micawber and Heep, of Pecksniff and Tapley, or of Chadband and Bucket could be transposed without wholly altering the impression of the characters which we derive from the nomenclature? Similarly, the genius of the great nonsense authors—Lear and Lewis Caroll—is shown in their choice of nonsense words. Who can describe a " Scroobious," or " Runcible " bird? Yet the man who does not at once grasp the fact that the outward appearance and special characteristics of these two birds must of necessity differ widely, will be wholly wanting in imagination. More, indeed, may be

[9]

said. A man of well-balanced mind, when he sees Lear's pictures, will forthwith say to himself: "Such is the appearance which I should naturally attribute to the Scroobious Bird. The Runcible Bird can obviously be like nothing else than that which is here depicted." Nothing, I should add, amused Lear more than the failure of some people to appreciate the utter absence of sense in his nonsense. He used to relate that some one once wrote to him to say that he had searched various botanical and other works without finding any allusion to a "Bong-tree."* Where, his correspondent, asked, did the "Bong-tree" grow?

Like Dickens in search of names, Lear was constantly manufacturing nonsense words. Practice made him proficient in the art. Here is a letter which he once wrote to me:

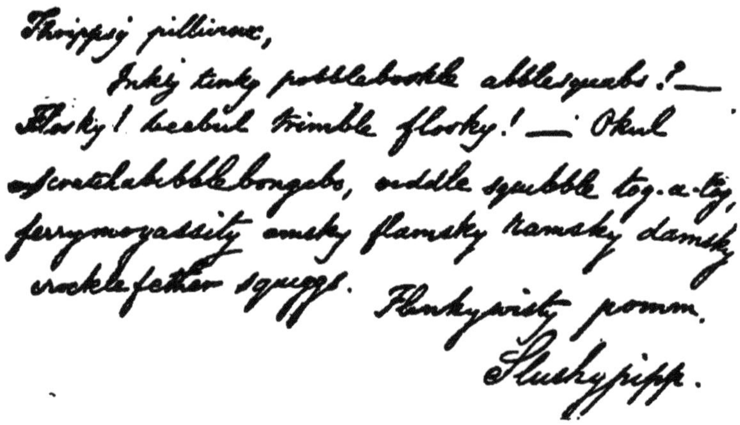
Thrippsy pillivinx,
Inky tinky pobblebockle abblesquabs?— Flosky! beebul trimble flosky!— Okul scratchabibblebongibo, viddle squibble tog-a-tog, ferrymoyassity amsky flamsky ramsky damsky crocklefether squiggs. Flinkywisty pomm.
Slushypipp.

* "They sailed away for a year and a day
To the land where the bong tree grows,
And there in a wood, a Piggiwig stood
With a ring at the end of his nose."
(*The Owl and the Pussy-Cat.*)

PREFACE

I hasten to add, for the benefit of anyone possessed of the mental endowments of him who asked for information about the " Bong-tree " that I believe " Slusshypipp " to be a wholly imaginary individual.

A poet who wrote in that language with which Lear's acquaintance was, indeed, imperfect, but the literature of which, nevertheless, whether in its ancient or modern form, constituted one of the delights and solaces of his life, once said that Poverty alone awoke the arts, and was the teacher of labour:

> Δ' πεγίο Διόφαγτε, χιδγα τὰς τέχγας ἐγείρει,
> ἀυτὰ τῦ χιόχθοιο διδάδχαλος. *

It is to that chill penury against which Lear's life was one continuous and arduous struggle, that we probably owe productions which have been the delight of so many nurseries. He perhaps occasionally felt some slight disappointment that his fame rested not so much on his merits as an artist, as on the fact that he was known throughout the child-world as the author of " Dumbledownderry." But neither his impecuniosity nor his disappointment could sour his essentially lovable nature, or tinge with the least shade of cynicism a humour, which was above all things kindly and genial. He was too warm-hearted to be satirical. His laughter was, indeed, akin to tears. I have known him sit down to the piano and sob whilst he played and sang: " Tears, Idle Tears," which he had himself set to music, and the next morning send me the subjoined sketch,

* Theocritus, Idyll xxl. 1.

[11]

PREFACE

accompanied by the following literary production, in which he
poked fun at his favourite poet and devoted friend:

> " Nluv, fluv bluv, ffluv biours,
>   Faith nunfaith kneer beekwl powers
>   Unfaith naught zwant a faith in all."

I give the following letters, which I have preserved and
which are illustrative of Lear's peculiar epistolary style:

PREFACE

BENEFICIAL AND BRICKLIKE BARING,—

Thank you for your note. I will come to His Excellency to-morry. Meanwhile, please give him the accompanying Note & Book, which I hope he & you & Strahan will like.

Give my love to Strahan.*

χαίρε - φιλέμου
'Ο Θδοάρδος λΰαρ

DEAR BARING,— *Toosdy.*

Disgustical to say, I must beg you to thank His Excellency from me, & to relate that I cannot come. I was engaged to dine with the De Verre's,† but am too unwell with awful cold in the head & eyes to go out at all.

* Captain (subsequently Sir George) Strahan and myself were Aides-de-Camp to Sir Henry Storks, who, at the time these letters were written, was Lord High Commissioner of the Ionian Islands.

† Major De Vere, Royal Engineers, was subsequently shot dead by one of his own men.

[18]

PREFACE

I have sent for 2 large tablecloths to blow my nose on, having already used up all my handkerchiefs. And altogether I am so unfit for company that I propose getting into a bag and being hung up to a bough of a tree till this tyranny is overpast. Please give the serming I send to His Excellency.

Yours sincerely,

EDWARD LEAR.

PREFACE

The aged & obese Landscape-
=painter will rejoice to come
to H. Excellency tomorrow —
he hopes EB RAADC* will go
to Athens next Monday weak

DEAR BARING,—

I ain't been out yet, but nevertheless will come to His Ex
cellency to-morrow evening—if snuffling & snorting & shiver
ing may be overlooked. If I had been out, I should hav
written my name at the Palace, which, as yet, I haven't had
the possibility of doing as decent folk should.

Did you ever see such a lot of brutal sno as is on Salva

[16]

dor?* Ain't it beastly. Generally speaking, I have been wrapped up like this all the week in a

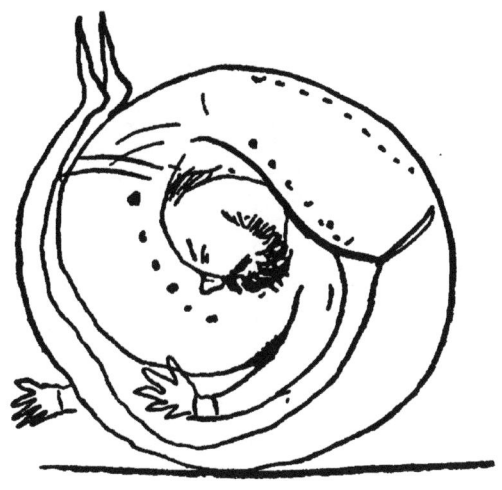

wholly abject and incapable state. . . .
Will you like to read " Le Maudit " ?—3 vols.
Yours sincerely,
EDW. LEAR.

* Saint Salvador is the name of the highest mountain in Corfû.

PREFACE

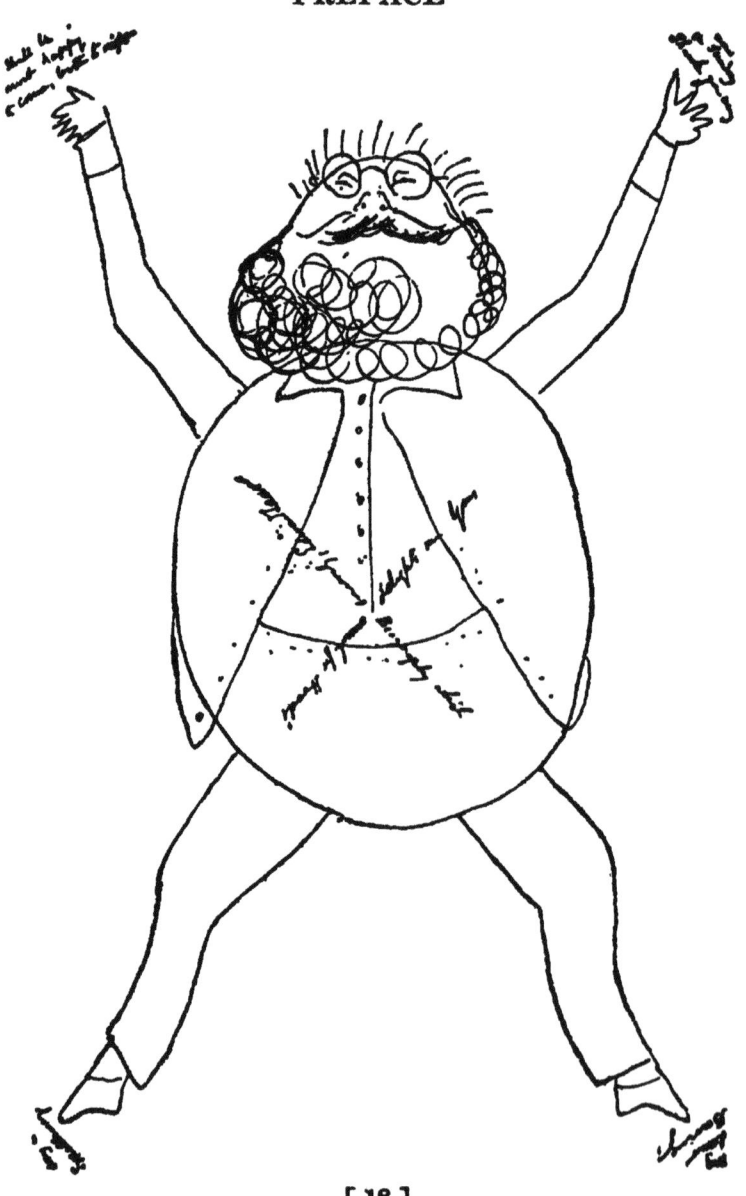

PREFACE

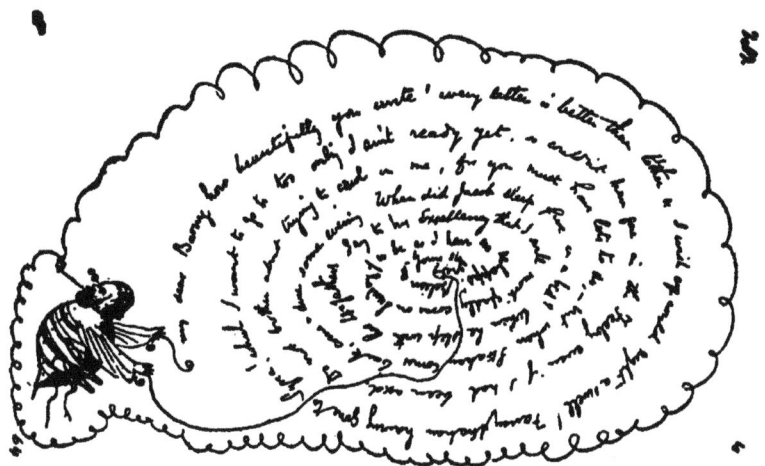

On one occasion, in conversation with Lear, one or other of us quoted the well-known lines in "Hudibras," in which allusion is made to "the learned Tabacotius" and the surgical operation which is connected with his name. We were neither of us quite sure whether we had quoted the last lines correctly. On the following morning Lear sent me this letter:

"Correction for the last lines of the quotation from Hewdybrass.

'But what the porter's life waned out
Off dropt the sympathetic snout.'"

PREFACE

PREFACE

15, STRATFORD PLACE, W.
30 *June,* 1864.

DEAR BARING,—

You see by the above that the Trunk has at last arrived:
—and queer enough—it had never been opened! so that every
one of my letters was just as it was, & everythink else—from
2 chocolate drops to an ounce of flea powder—was as it was
before the fathers fell asleep.

So, my dear boy, you are really off to-morrow! * I wish
you heartily a pleasant trip, and shall much like to hear from
you. Now don't get shot, & don't marry a squaw. You'd
better take out " Viscount Kirkwall's " book to amuse you on
the way. I meant to have got a portemonnaie or a cigar case
to leave at 11, Berkeley Sqr. as a memorial of old Corfû days
—but I fear I shan't have time now. But I shall hope to see
you when you come back—before Septbr. is out—or earlier.
For myself, I am all undecided as yet about winter plans.

The Treasurer & Mrs. Boyd & Charlie were with me to-
day, all flourishing. She is a kind-hearted woman. Boyd
showed me χαλολεράῶς letter which you told me of.

You were a good boy to write. Some day we may all
meet at Mollter. Goodbye.

Yours sincerely,
EDWARD LEAR.

When my eldest son was about three years old, his mother
expressed a wish that he should acquire some knowledge of
colour. Lear, with his usual kindness, at once sent twenty
drawings of birds of various colours—including, of course, his
favourites, the Scroobious and the Runcible birds. I had these
bound in a book. They are reproduced in this work.

* I was about to start for America to be a spectator for a short while of
the great war then in course of progress.

[21]

PREFACE

Many of the stories which Lear used to relate of his travels were extremely amusing. I give one of them. It may possibly have been already included in one of his published works, but, in any case, it will bear repetition.

Some fifty years ago, Lord Palmerston, by reason of the support he afforded to constitutional forms of government, was extremely unpopular amongst all those, on the Continent of Europe, who favoured the continuance of autocratic rule. This unpopularity gave rise to the well-known couplet—I think of Viennese manufacture:—

> " Hat der Teufel einen Sohn
> So ist er sicher Palmerston." *

Nowhere was he more unpopular than in the Kingdom of Naples, then ruled, or perhaps it would be more correct to say misruled, by Ferdinand II. (Bomba.) Lear was on one occasion sketching near a village in some remote part of Calabria. He was accosted by a gendarme, who requested him to show his passport. On seeing the signature of Palmerston at the bottom of the document, the gendarme thought that he had made an important capture. He arrested Lear and marched him into the village waving the passport which he carried in his hand, and shouting " Ho preso Palmerstone!"

86, WIMPOLE STREET.

* " If the Devil had a son,
Surely he'd be Palmerston."

[22]

EDITOR'S NOTE

AFTER the publication of my book of "Letters of Edward Lear" to my aunt and uncle, Lady Waldegrave and Lord Carlingford, in November, 1907, Lord Cromer most kindly put at my disposal, if I chose to use it, the "Bird Book" now included in this volume. A third edition of the "Letters" being about to be published, about June, 1908, it suggested itself to me that a short preface from such an old friend of Mr. Lear's would be of great value, and I ventured to ask Lord Cromer if he would be so good as to write something of this nature. As time was pressing I mentioned the fact to him, and with his characteristic promptitude he wrote: "Sunday I will look out my material, Monday I will write my preface, and Tuesday you shall have it." And it came as promised, but in such a form, that I felt the sin of wasting it as an additional preface to my old book.

So I at once resolved that Lord Cromer's delightful preface and unique Bird Book, should be the foundation of the new Nonsense Book I had for a long time contemplated and now made possible by Lord Cromer's very generous contributions. I myself had a few unpublished drawings originally belonging to my uncle; these have been most kindly supplemented by the following old friends of Mr. Lear. Mrs. W. Vaughan (Miss Madge Symonds), a cousin of my husband's and wife of the present Head Master of Wellington College, has allowed me to publish a large store of nonsense drawings drawn mostly, I believe, for her eldest sister Janet, and preserved with much care by their mother, Mrs. John Addington Symonds:—

[23]

"Lear dancing."
"Mrs. Blue Dickey-bird."
"High Diddle Diddle."
"Sing a Song of Sixpence."
Three unpublished illustrations for "The Owl and the Pussy Cat."
Miss Lushington:—
    "Spots of Greece."
The Earl of Northbrook:—
    "Mrs. Jaypher."
The Revd. Canon Selwyn:—
    "Dingly Bank."
Mr. Hubert Congreve:—
    "In Medio Tutorissimus Ibis."
The Earl of Cromer:—
    "The Bird Book."
    "Beneath these high Cathedral Stairs."
Mr. Henry Strachey:—
    Four lines of another version of "Mrs. Jaypher."

To all the above my thanks are due for their help in this latest tribute to the immortal writer of the Books of Nonsense.

CONSTANCE STRACHEY.

Sutton Court, September, 1911.

The new title, I would add, is taken from a letter of Lear to my uncle, in which he talks of "Queery Leary Nonsense," and my publishers and myself have thought it good to use Lear's own words.

LEAR'S INTRODUCTION TO MORE NONSENSE
SONGS AND STORIES

IN offering this little book—the third of its kind—to the
public, I am glad to take the opportunity of recording
the pleasure I have received at the appreciation its predeces-
sors have met with, as attested by their wide circulation, and
by the universally kind notices of them from the Press. To
have been the means of administering innocent mirth to thousands, may surely be a just motive for satisfaction, and an
excuse for grateful expression.

At the same time, I am desirous of adding a few words
as to the history of the two previously published volumes, and
more particularly of the first or original "Book of Nonsense,"
relating to which many absurd reports have crept into circulation, such as that it was the composition of the late Lord
Brougham, the late Earl of Derby, etc.; that the rhymes and
pictures are by different persons; or that the whole have a
symbolical meaning, etc.; whereas, every one of the Rhymes
was composed by myself, and every one of the Illustrations
drawn by my own hand at the time the verses were made.
Moreover, in no portion of these Nonsense drawings have I
ever allowed any caricature of private or public persons to
appear, and throughout, more care than might be supposed has
been given to make the subjects incapable of misinterpreta-
tion: "Nonsense," pure and absolute, having been my aim
throughout.

As for the persistently absurd report of the late Earl of
Derby being the author of the "First Book of Nonsense," I
may relate an incident which occurred to me four summers
ago, the first that gave me any insight into the origin of the
rumour.

[25]

INTRODUCTION

I was on my way from London to Guildford, in a railway carriage, containing, besides myself, one passenger, an elderly gentleman: presently, however, two ladies entered, accompanied by two little boys. These, who had just had a copy of the "Book of Nonsense" given them, were loud in their delight, and by degrees infected the whole party with their mirth.

"How grateful," said the old gentleman to the two ladies, "all children, and parents too, ought to be to the statesman who has given his time to composing that charming book!"

(The ladies looked puzzled, as indeed was I, the author.)

"Do you know who is the writer of it?" asked the gentleman.

"The name is 'Edward Lear,'" said one of the ladies.

"Ah!" said the first speaker, "so it is printed; but that is only a whim of the real author, the Earl of Derby. 'Edward' is his Christian name, and, as you may see, LEAR is only EARL transposed."

"But," said the lady, doubtingly, "here is a dedication to the great-grandchildren, grand-nephews, and grand-nieces of Edward, thirteenth Earl of Derby, by the author, Edward Lear."

"That," replied the other, "is simply a piece of mystification; I am in a position to know that the whole book was composed and illustrated by Lord Derby himself. In fact, there is no such a person at all as Edward Lear."

"Yet," said the other lady, "some friends of mine tell me they know Mr. Lear."

"Quite a mistake! completely a mistake!" said the old gentleman, becoming rather angry at the contradiction; "I am well aware of what I am saying: I can inform you, no such a person as 'Edward Lear' exists!"

Hitherto I had kept silence; but as my hat was, as well as my handkerchief and stick, largely marked inside with my name, and as I happened to have in my pocket several letters addressed to me, the temptation was too great to resist; so, flashing all these articles at once on my would-be extinguisher's attention, I speedily reduced him to silence.

The second volume of Nonsense, commencing with the verses, " The Owl and the Pussy-Cat," was written at different times, and for different sets of children: the whole being collected in the course of last year, were then illustrated, and published in a single volume, by Mr. R. J. Bush, of 32 Charing Cross.

The contents of the third or present volume were made also at different intervals in the last two years.

Long years ago, in days when much of my time was passed in a country house, where children and mirth abounded, the lines beginning, " There was an old man of Tobago," were suggested to me by a valued friend, as a form of verse lending itself to limitless variety for rhymes and pictures; and thenceforth the greater part of the original drawings and verses for the first " Book of Nonsense " were struck off with a pen, no assistance ever having been given me in any way but that of uproarious delight and welcome at the appearance of every new absurdity.

Most of these Drawings and Rhymes were transferred to lithographic stones in the year 1846, and were then first published by Mr. Thomas McLean, of the Haymarket. But that edition having been soon exhausted, and the call for the " Book of Nonsense " continuing, I added a considerable number of subjects to those previously published, and having caused the whole to be carefully reproduced in woodcuts by Messrs. Dalzell, I disposed of the copyright to Messrs. Routledge and Warne, by whom the volume was published in 1848.

EDWARD LEAR.

VILLA EMILY, SAN REMO,
August, 1871.

THE COMPLETE NONSENSE
BOOK

QUEERY LEARY NONSENSE

Mrs. Blue Dickey-bird, who went out a-walking with her six chickey-birds: she carried a parasol and wore a bonnet of green silk.

The first little chickey bird had daisies growing out of his head and wore boots because of the dirt.

The second little chickey bird wore a hat for fear it should rain.

The third little chickey bird carried a jug of water.

The fourth little chickey bird carried a muff, to keep her wings warm.

The fifth little chickey bird was round as a ball.

And the sixth little chickey bird walked on his head to save his feet.

[33]

High diddle diddle
The Cat, & the fiddle.

The Cow jumped over the moon.

The little dog laughed to see such sport.

And the dish ran away with the spoon

I sing a song of Sixpence, a Bag full of Rye,
Four & twenty blackbirds baked in a pie:

When the pie was opened the Birds began to sing

And wasn't that a dainty dish to set before the King?

The King was in his country house, Counting out his money.

The Queen was in the parlor, eating bread & honey,

The maid was in the garden
hanging out the clothes

When down came a blackbird & pecked
off her nose.

And shortly after that, there came a little wren,
As she sat upon a chair, & put it on again.

These three illustrations for the well-known rhyme " The Owl and the Pussy Cat " by Lear have not been published before.

One evening after dinner when on a visit to Lady Waldegrave and Lord Carlingford at Chewton Priory, Lear drew
the above parrot, a species of bird with which he was well acquainted, having illustrated the bird section of Lord Derby's
" Knowsley Menagerie."   After he had finished it Ward Braham, Lady Waldegrave's brother, drew the caricature of bird
and artist, reproduced on page 43, which amused Lear greatly.

[42]

The Spectacled Owlet

Jargon Bird

A caricature by Ward Braham, Lady Waldegrave's brother,
of Edward Lear singing.

Edward Lear's companion for years, and of which he made
many ridiculous pictures.

[Ger-woman loq.—Oh! I have my baby in the water dropped!
and I think that it drowned will be.

Ger-man loq.—That is natural: it is here so deep!!

Little-paper, moral and proverbial nonsense-illustrate on.]

Mr. Lear had a dislike of Germans, but it was accentuated by the hotel
which dominated and eventually ruined his beautiful Villa Emily at San
Remo, having been built and run by that race.

The above was probably drawn and sent off to his friend Fortescue at a
moment when this fact was strong in his mind.

AT DINGLE BANK

HE lived at Dingle Bank—he did;—
     He lived at Dingle bank;
And in his garden was one Quail,
   Four tulips, and a Tank;
And from his windows he could see
The otion and the River Dee.

His house stood on a Cliff,—it did,
   In aspic it was cool:
And many thousand little boys
   Resorted to his school,
Where if of progress they could boast
He gave them heaps of buttered toast.

But he grew rabid-wroth, he did,
   If they neglected books,
And dragged them to adjacent cliffs
   With beastly Button Hooks,
And there with fatuous glee he threw
Them down into the otion blue.

And in the sea they swam, they did,—
   All playfully about,
And some eventually became
   Sponges, or speckled trout:—
But Liverpool doth all bewail
Their Fate;—likewise his Garden Quail.

SPOTS OF GREECE

PAPA once went to Greece,
  And there I understand
He saw no end of lovely spots
  About that lovely land.
He talks about these spots of Greece
  To both Mama and me
Yet spots of Greece upon my dress
  They can't abear to see!
I cannot make it out at all—
  If ever on my Frock
They see the smallest Spot of Greece
  It gives them quite a shock!
Henceforth, therefore,—to please them both
  These spots of Greece no more
Shall be upon my frock at all—
  Nor on my Pinafore.

EPITAPH

"Beneath these high Cathedral stairs
  Lie the remains of Susan Pares.
  Her name was Wiggs, it was not Pares,
  But Pares was put to rhyme with stairs."

THE YOUTHFUL COVE

In medio Tutorissimus ibis.
" Thou shalt walk in the midst of the Tutors."

ONCE on a time a youthful cove
  As was a cheery lad
Lived in a villa by the sea.—
  The cove was not so bad;

The dogs and cats, the cows and ass,
  The birds in cage or grove,
The rabbits, hens, ducks, pony, pigs
  All loved that cheery lad.

Seven folks—one female and six male,—
  Seized on that youthful cove;
They said—" To edjukate this chap
  Us seven it doth behove."

The first his parrient was,—who taught
  The cove to read and ride,
Latin, and Grammarithemetic,
  And lots of things beside.

Says Pa, " I'll spare no pains or time
  Your school hours so to cut,
And square and fit, that you will make
  No end of progress—*but*—,"

Says Mrs. Grey,—" I'll teach him French,
  'Pour parler dans cette pays—
Je cris, qu'il parlera bien,
  Même comme un Francais—*Mais*—"

[49]

Says Signor Gambinossi,—" Si;
  Progresso si farà,
Lo voglio insegnare qui,
  La lingua mia,—ma,"—

Says Mr. Grump—" Geology,
  And Mathetics stiff
I'll teach the cove, who's sure to go
  Ahead like blazes,—*if*—"

Says James—" I'll teach him everyday
  My Nastics: now and then
To stand upon his 'ed; and make
  His mussels harder,—when "—

Says Signor Blanchi,—" Lascia far;—
  La musica da me,
Ben insegnata qli serà;—
  Farà progresso,—*Se*—"

Says Edmund Lear—" I'll make him draw
  A Palace, or a hut,
Trees, mountains, rivers, cities, plains,
  And p'rapps to paint them—*but*—"

So all these 7 joined hands and sang
  This chorus by the sea;—
" O! Ven his edjukation's done,
  By! Vot a cove he'll be!"

MRS. JAYPHER

A Preface to a poem entitled " Mrs. Jaypher." Lear adds the stage direction that the verse is to be read " sententiously and with grave importance."

MRS. JAYPHER found a wafer
   Which she struck upon a note;
This she took and gave the cook.
Then she went and bought a boat
Which she paddled down the stream
Shouting, " Ice produces cream,
Beer when churned produces butter!
Henceforth all the words I utter
Distant ages thus shall note—
' From the Jaypher Wisdom-Boat.' "

A VERSE OF ANOTHER VERSION

Mrs. Jaypher said its safer
If you've lemons in your head
First to eat a pound of meat
And then to go at once to bed.

THE BOOK OF NONSENSE

There was an Old Man with a nose,
Who said, "If you choose to suppose
That my nose is too long, you are certainly wrong!"
That remarkable Man
    with a nose.

There was a Young Person of Smyrna,
Whose Grandmother threatened to burn her;
But she seized on the Cat, and said, " Granny, burn that!
You incongruous Old Woman of Smyrna!"

There was an Old Man on a hill,
Who seldom, if ever, stood still;
He ran up and down in his Grandmother's gown,
Which adorned that Old Man on a hill.

There was an Old Person of Chili,
Whose conduct was painful and silly;
He sate on the stairs, eating apples and pears,
That imprudent Old Person of Chili.

[56]

There was an Old Man of Kilkenny,
Who never had more than a penny;
He spent all that money in onions and honey,
That wayward Old Man
of Kilkenny.

There was an Old Man with a gong,
Who bumped at it all the day long;
But they called out, " Oh, law! you're a horrid old bore! "
So they smashed that Old Man with a gong.

[57]

There was an Old Man of Columbia,
Who was thirsty, and called out for some beer;
But they brought it quite hot, in a small copper pot,
Which disgusted that man of Columbia.

There was an Old Man in a tree,
Who was horribly bored by a Bee;
When they said, " Does it buzz? " he replied, " Yes, it does!
It's a regular brute of a Bee."

[58]

There was an Old Lady of Chertsey,
Who made a remarkable curtsey;
She twirled round and round, till she sank underground,
Which distressed all the people of Chertsey.

There was a Young Lady whose chin
Resembled the point of a pin;
So she had it made sharp, and purchased a harp,
And played several tunes with her chin.

[59]

There was an Old Man with a flute,—
A "sarpint" ran into his boot!
But he played day and night,
    till the "sarpint" took
      flight,
And avoided that Man
    with a flute.

There was a Young Lady of Portugal,
Whose ideas were excessively nautical;
She climbed up a tree to examine the sea,
But declared she would never leave Portugal.

[60]

There was an Old Person of Ischia,
Whose conduct grew friskier and friskier;
He danced hornpipes and jigs, and ate thousands of figs,
That lively old Person of Ischia.

There was an Old Man of Vienna,
Who lived upon Tincture of Senna;
When that did not agree, he took Camomile Tea,
That nasty Old Man of Vienna.

There was an Old Man in a boat,
Who said, " I'm afloat! I'm afloat!"
When they said, " No, you ain't!" he was ready to faint,
That unhappy Old Man in a boat.

There was an Old Person of Buda,
Whose conduct grew ruder and ruder,
Till at last with a hammer they silenced his clamor,
By smashing that Person of Buda.

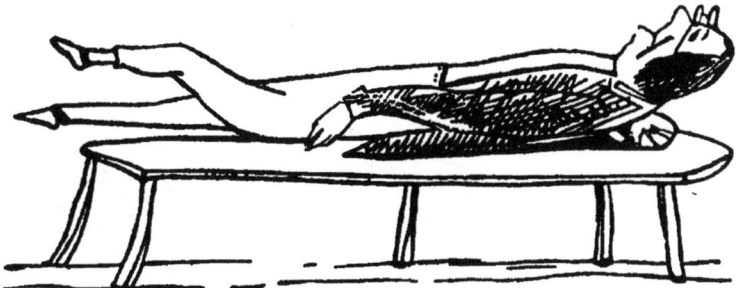

There was an Old Man of Moldavia,
Who had the most curious behaviour;
For while he was able, he slept on a table,
That funny Old Man
    of Moldavia.

There was an Old Person of Hurst,
Who drank when he was not athirst;
When they said, " You'll grow fatter! " he answered " What
    matter? "   That globular Person of Hurst.

There was an Old Man of Madras,
Who rode on a cream-coloured Ass;
But the length of its ears so promoted his fears,
That it killed that Old Man of Madras.

There was an Old Person of Dover,
Who rushed through a field of blue clover;
But some very large Bees stung his nose and his knees,
So he very soon went back to Dover.

There was an Old Person of Cadiz,
Who was always polite to all ladies;
But in handling his daughter, he fell into the water,
Which drowned that Old
    Person of Cadiz.

There was an Old Person of Leeds,
Whose head was infested with beads;
She sat on a stool and ate gooseberry-fool,
Which agreed with that Person of Leeds.

There was an Old
  Man of the Isles,
Whose face was pervaded with smiles;
He sang " High dum diddle," and played on the fiddle,
That amiable Man
  of the Isles.

There was an Old Person of Basing,
Whose presence of mind was amazing;
He purchased a steed, which he rode at full speed,
And escaped from the people of Basing.

There was an Old Man who supposed
That the street door was partially closed;
But some very large Rats ate his coats and his hats,
While that futile Old Gentleman dozed.

There was an Old Person whose habits
Induced him to feed upon Rabbits;
When he'd eaten eighteen, he turned perfectly green,
Upon which he relinquished those habits.

[67]

There was an Old Man of the West,
Who wore a pale plum-coloured vest;
When they said, "Does it fit?" he replied, "Not a bit!"
That uneasy Old Man of the West.

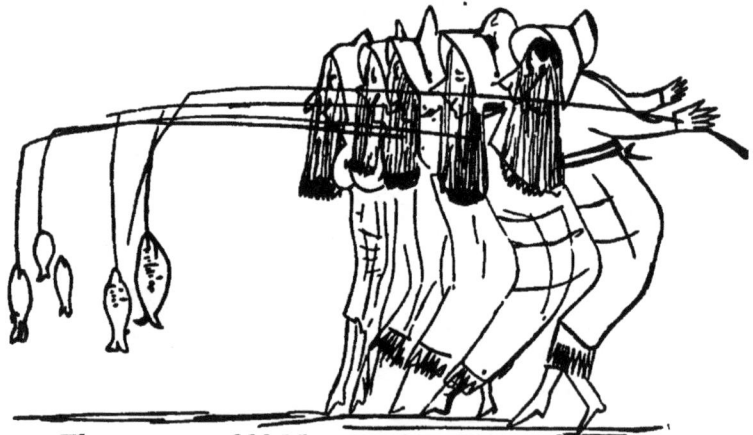

There was an Old Man of Marseilles,
Whose daughters wore bottle-green veils;
They caught several Fish, which they put in a dish,
And sent to their Pa at Marseilles.

There was an Old Man of the Wrekin,
Whose shoes made a horrible creaking;
But they said, " Tell us whether your shoes are of leather,
Or of what, you Old Man of the Wrekin?"

There was a Young Lady whose nose
Was so long that it reached to her toes;
So she hired an Old Lady, whose conduct was steady,
To carry that wonderful nose.

[69]

There was an Old Man of Apulia,
Whose conduct was very peculiar;
He fed twenty sons upon nothing but buns,
That whimsical Man of Apulia.

There was an Old Man of Quebec,—
A beetle ran over his neck;
But he cried, " With a needle I'll slay you, O beadle!"
That angry Old Man of Quebec.

There was a Young Lady of Norway,
Who casually sat in a doorway;
When the door squeezed her flat, she exclaimed, " What of
    that? "
This courageous Young Lady
    of Norway.

There was a Young Lady of Bute,
Who played on a silver-gilt flute;
She played several jigs to her Uncle's white Pigs:
That amusing Young Lady of Bute.

There was an Old Person of Philæ,
Whose conduct was scroobious and wily;
He rushed up a Palm when the weather was calm,
And observed all the ruins of Philæ.

There was an Old Man with a poker,
Who painted his face with red ochre.
When they said, " You're a Guy! " he made no reply,
But knocked them all down with his poker.

There was an Old Man of Peru,
Who watched his wife making a stew;
But once, by mistake, in a stove she did bake
That unfortunate Man of Peru.

There was an Old Person of Prague,
Who was suddenly seized with the plague;
But they gave him some butter, which caused him to mutter,
And cured that Old Person of Prague.

There was an Old Man of the North,
Who fell into a basin of broth;
But a laudable cook fished him out with a hook,
Which saved that Old Man of the North.

There was an Old Person of Troy,
Whose drink was warm brandy and soy,
Which he took with a spoon, by the light of the moon,
In sight of the city of Troy.

There was an Old Man of Melrose,
Who walked on the tips of his toes;
But they said, " It ain't pleasant to see you at present,
You stupid Old Man of Melrose."

There was an Old Person of Tring,
Who embellished his nose with a ring;
He gazed at the moon every evening in June,
That ecstatic Old Person of Tring.

[75]

There was an Old Person of Mold,
Who shrank from sensations of cold;
So he purchased some muffs, some furs, and some fluffs,
And wrapped himself well from the cold.

There was an Old Man of the Nile,
Who sharpened his nails with a file,
Till he cut off his thumbs, and said calmly, " This comes
Of sharpening one's nails with a file! "

There was an Old Man of Nepaul,
From his horse had a terrible fall;
But, though split quite in two, with some very strong glue
They mended that man of Nepaul.

There was an Old Man of th' Abruzzi,
So blind that he couldn't his foot see;
When they said, " That's your toe," he replied, " Is it so?"
That doubtful Old Man of th' Abruzzi.

There was an Old Man of Calcutta,
Who perpetually ate bread and butter;
Till a great bit of muffin, on which he was stuffing,
Choked that horrid Old Man of Calcutta.

There was an Old Person of Rhodes,
Who strongly objected to toads;
He paid several cousins to catch them by dozens,
That futile Old Person of Rhodes.

[79]

There was an Old Man of the South,
Who had an immoderate mouth;
But in swallowing a dish that was quite full of Fish,
He was choked, that Old Man of the South.

There was an Old Man of the Dee,
Who was sadly annoyed by a Flea;
When he said, " I will scratch it! " they gave him a hatchet,
Which grieved that Old Man of the Dee.

There was a Young Lady of Lucca,
Whose lovers completely forsook her;
She ran up a tree, and said " Fiddle-de-dee! "
Which embarrassed the people of Lucca.

[81]

There was an Old Man of Coblenz,
The length of whose legs was immense;
He went with one prance from Turkey to France,
That surprising Old Man of Coblenz.

There was an Old Man of Bohemia,
Whose daughter was christened Euphemia;
But one day, to his grief, she married a thief,
Which grieved that Old Man of Bohemia.

There was an Old Man of Corfu,
Who never knew what he should do;
So he rushed up and down, till the sun made him brown,
That bewildered Old Man of Corfu.

There was an Old Man of Vesuvius,
Who studied the works of Vitruvius;
When the flames burnt his book, to drinking he took,
That morbid Old Man of Vesuvius.

There was an Old Man of Dundee,
Who frequented the top of a tree;
When disturbed by the Crows, he abruptly arose,
And exclaimed, " I'll return to Dundee! "

There was an Old Lady whose folly
Induced her to sit in a holly;
Whereon, by a thorn her dress being torn,
She quickly became melancholy.

There was an Old Man on some rocks,
Who shut his Wife up in a box:
When she said, " Let me out," he exclaimed, " Without doubt
You will pass all your life in that box."

There was an Old Person of Rheims,
Who was troubled with horrible dreams;
So to keep him awake they fed him with cake,
Which amused that Old Person of Rheims.

There was an Old Man of Leghorn,
The smallest that ever was born;
But quickly snapt up he was once by a Puppy,
Who devoured that Old Man of Leghorn.

There was an Old Man in a pew,
Whose waistcoat was spotted with blue;
But he tore it in pieces, to give to his Nieces,
That cheerful Old Man in a pew.

[87]

There was a Young Lady of Hull,
Who was chased by a virulent Bull;
But she seized on a spade, and called out, " Who's afraid? "
Which distracted that virulent Bull.

There was an Old Person of Dutton,
Whose head was as small as a button;
So to make it look big he purchased a wig,
And rapidly rushed about Dutton.

There was a Young Lady of Troy,
Whom several large flies did annoy;
Some she killed with a thump, some she drowned at the pump,
And some she took with her to Troy.

There was an Old Man who said, "How
Shall I flee from this horrible Cow?
I will sit on this stile, and continue to smile,
Which may soften the heart of that Cow."

[89]

There was an Old Person of Bangor,
Whose face was distorted with anger;
He tore off his boots, and subsisted on roots,
That borascible Person of Bangor.

There was an Old Man who said, " Hush!
I perceive a young bird in this bush!"
When they said, " Is it small?" he replied, " Not at all;
It is four times as big as the bush!"

There was a Young Lady of Russia,
Who screamed so that no one could hush her;
Her screams were extreme,—no one heard such a scream
As was screamed by that Lady of Russia.

There was a Young Lady of Tyre,
Who swept the loud chords of a lyre;
At the sound of each sweep she enraptured the deep,
And enchanted the city of Tyre.

[91]

There was an Old Man of Jamaica,
Who suddenly married a Quaker;
But she cried out, " Oh, lack! I have married a black! "
Which distressed that Old Man of Jamaica.

There was an Old Man of the East,
Who gave all his children a feast;
But they all ate so much, and their conduct was such
That it killed that Old Man of the East.

There was an Old Man of the Coast,
Who placidly sat on a post;
But when it was cold he relinquished his hold,
And called for some hot buttered toast.

There was an Old Man of Kamschatka,
Who possessed a remarkably fat Cur;
His gait and his waddle were held as a model
To all the fat dogs in Kamschatka.

There was an Old Person of Gretna,
Who rushed down the crater of Etna;
When they said, " Is it hot? " he replied, " No, it's not! "
That mendacious Old Person of Gretna.

There was an Old Person of Tartary,
Who divided his jugular artery;
But he screeched to his Wife, and she said, " Oh, my life!
Your death will be felt by all Tartary! "

There was an Old Man of Berlin,
Whose form was uncommonly thin;
Till he once, by mistake, was mixed up in a cake,
So they baked that Old Man of Berlin.

There was an Old Man of the West,
Who never could get any rest;
So they set him to spin on his nose and his chin,
Which cured that Old Man of the West.

[95]

There was an Old Person of Cheadle
Was put in the stocks by the Beadle
For stealing some pigs, some coats, and some wigs,
That horrible person of Cheadle.

There was an Old Person of Anerley,
Whose conduct was strange and unmannerly;
He rushed down the Strand with a Pig in each hand,
But returned in the evening to Anerley.

[96]

There was an Old Man of Whitehaven,
Who danced a quadrille with a Raven;
But they said, " It's absurd to encourage this bird! "
So they smashed that Old Man of Whitehaven.

There was a Young Lady of Wales,
Who caught a large Fish without scales;
When she lifted her hook, she exclaimed, " Only look!"
That ecstatic Young Lady of Wales.

There was an Old Man with a beard,
Who sat on a Horse when he reared;
But they said, " Never mind! you will fall off behind,
You propitious Old Man with a beard!"

There was a Young Lady of Welling,
Whose praise all the world was a-telling;
She played on the harp, and caught several Carp,
That accomplished Young Lady of Welling.

There was a Young Lady of Sweden,
Who went by the slow train to Weedon;
When they cried, "Weedon Station!" she made no observa-
    tion,
But thought she should go back to Sweden.

There was an Old Person of Chester,
Whom several small children did pester;
They threw some large stones, which broke most of his bones,
And displeased that Old Person of Chester.

[101]

There was an Old Man of the Cape,
Who possessed a large Barbary Ape;
Till the Ape, one dark night, set the house all alight,
Which burned that Old Man of the Cape.

There was an Old Person of Burton,
Whose answers were rather uncertain;
When they said, "How d'ye do?" he replied, "Who are
    you?"
That distressing Old Person of Burton.

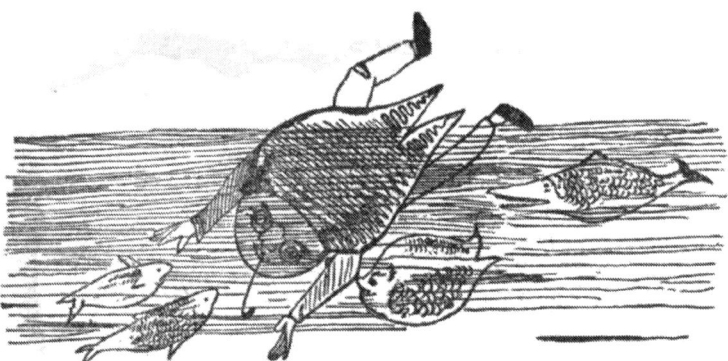

There was an Old Person of Ems
Who casually fell in the Thames;
And when he was found, they said he was drowned,
That unlucky Old Person of Ems.

There was an Old Lady of Prague,
Whose language was horribly vague;
When they said, " Are these caps? " she answered, " Perhaps! "
That oracular Lady of Prague.

There was a Young Lady of Poole,
Whose soup was excessively cool;
So she put it to boil by the aid of some oil,
That ingenious Young Lady of Poole.

There was a Young Girl of Majorca,
Whose Aunt was a very fast walker;
She walked seventy miles, and leaped fifteen stiles,
Which astonished that Girl of Majorca.

There was a Young Lady of Parma,
Whose conduct grew calmer and calmer;
When they said, "Are you dumb?" she merely said, "Hum!"
That provoking Young Lady of Parma.

There was an Old Person of Sparta,
Who had twenty-five sons and one "darter;"
He fed them on Snails, and weighed them in scales,
That wonderful Person of Sparta.

There was a Young Lady of Turkey,
Who wept when the weather was murky;
When the day turned out fine, she ceased to repine,
That capricious Young Lady of Turkey.

There was an Old Man on
  whose nose
Most birds of the
  air could repose;
But they all flew away at the closing of day,
Which relieved that Old Man and his nose.

There was an Old Man of Aôsta
Who possessed a large Cow, but he lost her;
But they said, " Don't you see she has run up a tree,
You invidious Old Man of Aôsta? "

There was a Young Person of Crete,
Whose toilette was far from complete;
She dressed in a sack spickle-speckled with black,
That ombliferous Person of Crete.

There was a Young Lady of Clare,
Who was madly pursued by a Bear;
When she found she was tired, she abruptly expired,
That unfortunate Lady of Clare.

There was a Young Lady of Dorking,
Who bought a large bonnet for walking;
But its color and size so bedazzled her eyes,
That she very soon went back to Dorking.

[110]

There was an Old Man of Cape Horn,
Who wished he had never been born;
So he sat on a Chair till he died of despair,
That dolorous Man of Cape Horn.

There was an Old Person of Cromer,
Who stood on one leg to read Homer;
When he found he grew stiff, he jumped over the cliff,
Which concluded that Person of Cromer.

There was an Old Man of the Hague,
Whose ideas were excessively vague;
He built a balloon to examine the moon,
That deluded Old Man of the Hague.

There was an Old Person of Spain,
Who hated all trouble and pain;
So he sate on a chair with his feet in the air,
That umbrageous Old Person of Spain.

There was an Old Man who said, " Well!
Will *nobody* answer this bell?
I have pulled day and night, till my hair has grown white,
But nobody answers this bell! "

There was an Old Man with an Owl,
Who continued to bother and howl;
He sat on a rail, and imbibed bitter ale,
Which refreshed that Old Man and his Owl.

There was an Old Man in a casement,
Who held up his hands in amazement;
When they said, " Sir, you'll fall!" he replied, " Not at all!"
That incipient Old Man in a casement.

There was an Old Person of Ewell,
Who chiefly subsisted on gruel;
But to make it more nice, he inserted some Mice,
Which refreshed that Old Person of Ewell.

There was an Old Man of Peru,
Who never knew what he should do;
So he tore off his hair, and behaved like a bear,
That intrinsic Old Man of Peru.

There was a Young Lady of Ryde,
Whose shoe-strings were seldom untied;
She purchased some clogs, and some small spotty Dogs,
And frequently walked about Ryde.

There was a Young Lady whose eyes
Were unique as to color and size;
When she opened them wide, people all turned aside,
And started away in surprise.

There was an Old Man with a beard,
Who said, "It is just as I feared!—
Two Owls and a Hen, four larks and a Wren,
Have all built their nests in my beard."

There was a Young Lady whose bonnet
Came untied when the birds sate upon it;
But she said, "I don't care! all the birds in the air
Are welcome to sit on my bonnet!"

NONSENSE SONGS AND STORIES

THE OWL AND THE PUSSY-CAT

I

THE Owl and the Pussy-Cat went to sea
　　In a beautiful pea-green boat:
They took some honey, and plenty of money
　　Wrapped up in a five-pound note.
The Owl looked up to the stars above,
　　And sang to a small guitar,
　"O lovely Pussy, O Pussy, my love,
　What a beautiful Pussy you are,
　　　　　You are,
　　　　　You are!
　What a beautiful Pussy you are!"

II

Pussy said to the Owl, " You elegant fowl,
　　How charmingly sweet you sing!
Oh! let us be married; too long we have tarried:
　　But what shall we do for a ring?"

They sailed away, for a year and a day,
  To the land where the bong-tree grows;
And there in a wood a Piggy-wig stood,
  With a ring at the end of his nose,

His nose,
His nose,
With a ring at the end of his nose.

III

" Dear Pig, are you willing to sell for one shilling
   Your ring?" Said the Piggy, "I will."
So they took it away, and were married next day
   By the Turkey who lives on the hill.
They dined on mince and slices of quince,
   Which they ate with a runcible spoon;
And hand in hand, on the edge of the sand
   They danced by the light of the moon,
         The moon,
         The moon,
   They danced by the light of the moon.

THE DUCK AND THE KANGAROO

I

SAID the Duck to the Kangaroo,
   "Good gracious! how you hop
Over the fields, and the water too,
   As if you never would stop!
My life is a bore in this nasty pond;
And I long to go out in the world beyond:
   I wish I could hop like you,"
   Said the Duck to the Kangaroo.

II

" Please give me a ride on your back,"
   Said the Duck to the Kangaroo:
" I would sit quite still, and say nothing but ' Quack,'
   The whole of the long day through;
And we'd go the Dee, and the Jelly Bo Lee,
Over the land, and over the sea:
   Please take me a ride! oh, do!"
   Said the Duck to the Kangaroo.

III

Said the Kangaroo to the Duck,
" This requires some little reflection.
Perhaps, on the whole, it might bring me luck:
   And there seems but one objection;
Which is, if you'll let me speak so bold,
Your feet are unpleasantly wet and cold,
   And would probably give me the roo—
   Matiz," said the Kangaroo.

IV

Said the Duck, " As I sate on the rocks,
   I have thought over that completely;

And I bought four pairs of worsted socks,
  Which fit my web-feet neatly;

And, to keep out the cold, I've bought a cloak;
And every day a cigar I'll smoke;
  All to follow my own dear true
  Love of a Kangaroo."

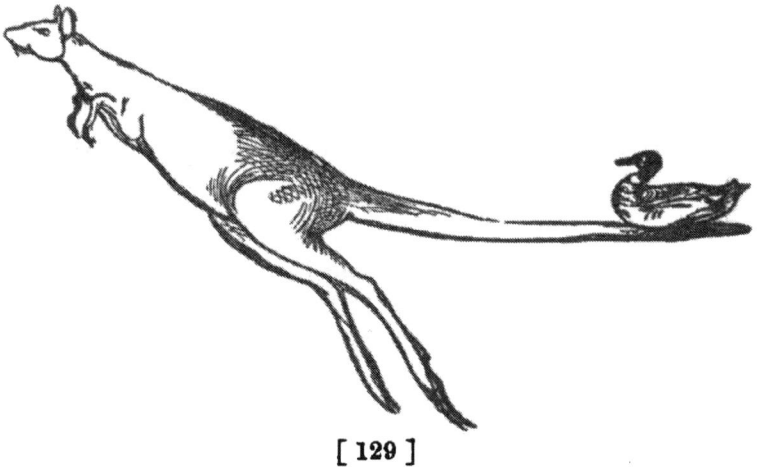

v

Said the Kangaroo, " I'm ready,
  All in the moonlight pale;
But to balance me well, dear Duck, sit steady,
  And quite at the end of my tail."

So away they went with a hop and a bound;
And they hopped the whole world three times round.
  And who so happy, oh! who,
  As the Duck and the Kangaroo?

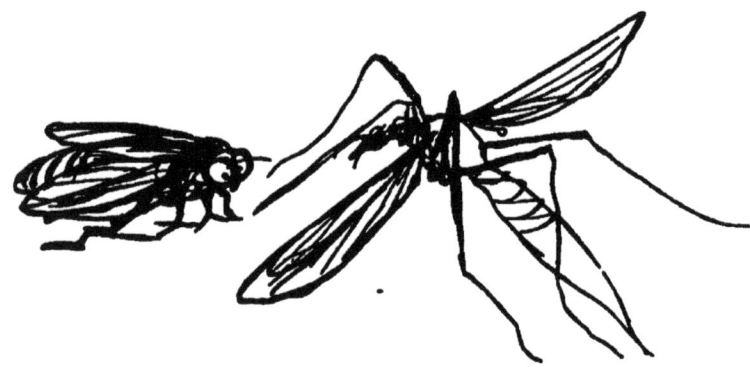

THE DADDY LONG-LEGS AND THE FLY

I

ONCE Mr. Daddy Long-Legs,
  Dressed in brown and gray,
Walked about upon the sands
  Upon a summer's day:
And there among the pebbles,
  When the wind was rather cold,

He met with Mr. Floppy Fly,
  All dressed in blue and gold;
And, as it was too soon to dine,
They drank some periwinkle-wine,
And played an hour or two, or more,
At battlecock and shuttledore.

II

Said Mr. Daddy Long-legs
  To Mr. Floppy Fly,
" Why do you never come to court?
  I wish you'd tell me why.
All gold and shine, in dress so fine,
  You'd quite delight the court.
Why do you never go at all?
  I really think you *ought*.
And, if you went, you'd see such sights!
Such rugs and jugs and candle-lights!
And, more than all, the king and queen,—
One in red, and one in green."

III

" O Mr. Daddy Long-legs! "
  Said Mr. Floppy Fly,
" It's true I never go to court;
  And I will tell you why.
If I had six long legs like yours,
  At once I'd go to court;
But, oh! I can't, because *my* legs
  Are so extremely short.
And I'm afraid the king and queen
(One in red, and one in green)
Would say aloud, ' You are not fit,
You Fly, to come to court a bit!'

IV

"Oh, Mr. Daddy Long-legs!"
    Said Mr. Floppy Fly,
"I wish you'd sing one little song,
    One mumbian melody.
You used to sing so awful well
    In former days gone by;
But now you never sing at all:
    I wish you'd tell me why:
For, if you would, the silvery sound
Would please the shrimps and cockles round,
And all the crabs would gladly come
To hear you sing, 'Ah, Hum di Hum!'"

V

Said Mr. Daddy Long-legs,
    "I can never sing again;
And, if you wish, I'll tell you why,
    Although it gives me pain.
For years I cannot hum a bit,
    Or sing the smallest song;
And this the dreadful reason is,—
    My legs are grown too long!
My six long legs, all here and there,
Oppress my bosom with despair;
And, if I stand or lie or sit,
I cannot sing one single bit!"

VI

So Mr. Daddy Long-legs
    And Mr. Floppy Fly
Sat down in silence by the sea,
    And gazed upon the sky.

[132]

They said, " This is a dreadful thing!
  The world has all gone wrong,
Since one has legs too short by half,
  The other much too long.
One never more can go to court,
Because his legs have grown too short;
The other cannot sing a song,
Because his legs have grown too long!"

VII

Then Mr. Daddy Long-legs
  And Mr. Floppy Fly
Rushed downward to the foamy sea
  With one sponge-taneous cry:
And there they found a little boat,
  Whose sails were pink and grey;
And off they sailed among the waves,
  Far and far away:
They sailed across the silent main,
And reached the great Gromboolian Plain;
And there they play forevermore
At battlecock and shuttledore.

THE JUMBLIES

I

THEY went to sea in a sieve, they did;
  In a sieve they went to sea:
In spite of all their friends could say,
On a winter's morn, on a stormy day,
  In a sieve they went to sea.
And when the sieve turned round and round,
And every one cried, "You'll all be drowned!"
They called aloud, "Our sieve ain't big;
But we don't care a button, we don't care a fig:
  In a sieve we'll go to sea!"
      Far and few, far and few,
        Are the lands where the Jumblies live:
        Their heads are green, and their hands are blue;
        And they went to sea in a sieve.

II

They sailed away in a sieve, they did,
  In a sieve they sailed so fast,

With only a beautiful pea-green veil
Tied with a ribbon, by way of a sail,
  To a small tobacco-pipe mast.
And every one said who saw them go,
"Oh! won't they be soon upset, you know?
For the sky is dark, and the voyage is long;
And, happen what may, it's extremely wrong
  In a sieve to sail so fast."
      Far and few, far and few,
        Are the lands where the Jumblies live:
        Their heads are green, and their hands are blue;
        And they went to sea in a sieve.

                        III
The water it soon came in, it did;
  The water it soon came in:
So, to keep them dry, they wrapped their feet
In a pinky paper all folded neat;
  And they fastened it down with a pin.
And they passed the night in a crockery-jar;
And each of them said, "How wise we are!
Though the sky be dark, and the voyage be long,
Yet we never can think we were rash or wrong,
  While round in our sieve we spin."
      Far and few, far and few,
        Are the lands where the Jumblies live:
        Their heads are green, and their hands are blue;
        And they went to sea in a sieve.

                        IV
And all night long they sailed away;
  And when the sun went down,
They whistled and warbled a moony song

To the echoing sound of a coppery gong,
  In the shade of the mountains brown.
"O Timballoo! How happy we are
When we live in a sieve and a crockery-jar!
And all night long, in the moonlight pale,
We sail away with a pea-green sail
  In the shade of the mountains brown."
      Far and few, far and few,
          Are the lands where the Jumblies live:
          Their heads are green, and their hands are blue;
          And they went to sea in a sieve.

V

They sailed to the Western Sea, they did,—
  To a land all covered with trees:
And they bought an owl, and a useful cart,
And a pound of rice, and a cranberry-tart,
  And a hive of silvery bees;
And they bought a pig, and some green jackdaws,
And a lovely monkey with lollipop paws,
And forty bottles of ring-bo-ree,
  And no end of Stilton cheese.
      Far and few, far and few,
          Are the lands where the Jumblies live:
          Their heads are green, and their hands are blue;
          And they went to sea in a sieve.

VI

And in twenty years they all came back,—
  In twenty years or more;
And every one said, "How tall they've grown!
For they've been to the Lakes, and the Torrible Zone,
  And the hills of the Chankly Bore."
And they drank their health, and gave them a feast

Of dumplings made of beautiful yeast;
And every one said, " If we only live,
We, too, will go to sea in a sieve,
  To the hills of the Chankly Bore."
      Far and few, far and few,— PAUSE
        Are the lands where the Jumblies live:
        Their heads are green, and their hands are blue;
        And they went to sea in a sieve.

THE NUTCRACKERS AND THE SUGAR-TONGS

I

THE Nutcrackers sate by a plate on the table;
  The Sugar-tongs sate by a plate at his side;
And the Nutcrackers said, " Don't you wish we were able
  Along the blue hills and green meadows to ride?
Must we drag on this stupid existence forever,
  So idle and weary, so full of remorse,
While every one else takes his pleasure, and never
  Seems happy unless he is riding a horse?

II

" Don't you think we could ride without being instructed,
  Without any saddle or bridle or spur?
Our legs are so long, and so aptly constructed,
  I'm sure that an accident could not occur.
Let us all of a sudden hop down from the table,
  And hustle downstairs, and each jump on a horse!

Shall we try? Shall we go? Do you think we are able?"
 The Sugar-tongs answered distinctly, "Of course!"

III

So down the long staircase they hopped in a minute;
 The Sugar-tongs snapped, and the Crackers said "Crack!"
The stable was open; the horses were in it:
 Each took out a pony, and jumped on his back.
The Cat in a fright scrambled out of the doorway;
 The Mice tumbled out of a bundle of hay;
The brown and white Rats, and the black ones from Norway,
 Screamed out, "They are taking the horses away!"

IV

The whole of the household was filled with amazement:
The Cups and the Saucers danced madly about;
The Plates and the Dishes looked out of the casement;
 The Salt-cellar stood on his head with a shout;
The Spoons, with a clatter, looked out of the lattice;
 The Mustard-pot climbed up the gooseberry-pies;
The Soup-ladle peeped through a heap of veal-patties,
 And squeaked with a ladle-like scream of surprise.

V

The Frying-pan said, "It's an awful delusion!"
 The Tea-kettle hissed, and grew black in the face;
And they all rushed downstairs in the wildest confusion
 To see the great Nutcracker-Sugar-tong race.
And out of the stable, with screamings and laughter
 (Their ponies were cream-coloured, speckled with brown),
The Nutcrackers first, and the Sugar-tongs after,
 Rode all round the yard, and then all round the town.

VI

They rode through the street, and they rode by the station;
 They galloped away to the beautiful shore;

In silence they rode, and "made no observation,"
  Save this: "We will never go back any more!"
And still you might hear, till they rode out of hearing,
  The Sugar-tongs snap, and the Crackers say "Crack!"
Till, far in the distance their forms disappearing,
  They faded away; and they never came back!

CALICO PIE

I

CALICO pie,
  The little birds fly
Down to the calico-tree:
Their wings were blue,
And they sang "Tilly-loo!"
Till away they flew;
  And they never came back to me!

They never came back,
They never came back,
They never came back to me!

II

Calico jam,
The little Fish swam
Over the Syllabub Sea.
He took off his hat
To the Sole and the Sprat,
And the Willeby-wat:

But he never came back to me;
He never came back,
He never came back,
He never came back to me,

III

Calico ban,
The little Mice ran
To be ready in time for tea;
Flippity flup,
They drank it all up,

And danced in the cup:
But they never came back to me;
They never came back,
They never came back,
They never came back to me.

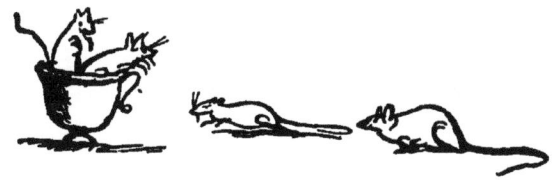

IV

Calico drum,
The Grasshoppers come,
The Butterfly, Beetle, and Bee,
Over the ground,
Around and round,
With a hop **and a bound**;

But they never came back,
They never came back,
They never came back,
They never came back to me.

MR. AND MRS. SPIKKY SPARROW

I

IN a little piece of wood
   Mr. Spikky Sparrow stood:
Mrs. Sparrow sate close by,
A-making of an insect-pie
For her little children five,
In the nest and all alive;
Singing with a cheerful smile,
To amuse them all the while,
      "Twikky wikky wikky wee,
      Wikky bikky twikky tee,
        Spikky bikky bee!"

II

Mrs. Spikky Sparrow said,
"Spikky, darling! in my head
Many thoughts of trouble come,
Like to flies upon a plum.
All last night, among the trees,
I heard you cough, I heard you sneeze;
And thought I, 'It's come to that
Because he does not wear a hat!'

Chippy wippy sikky tee,
Bikky wikky tikky mee,
Spikky chippy wee!

III

"Not that you are growing old;
But the nights are growing cold.
No one stays out all night long
Without a hat: I'm sure it's wrong!"
Mr. Spikky said, " How kind,
Dear, you are, to speak your mind!
All your life I wish you luck!
You are, you are, a lovely duck!
Witchy witchy witchy wee,
Twitchy witchy witchy bee,
Tikky tikky tee!

IV

"I was also sad, and thinking,
When one day I saw you winking,
And I heard you sniffle-snuffle,
And I saw your feathers ruffle:
To myself I sadly said,
' She's neuralgia in her head!
That dear head has nothing on it!
Ought she not to wear a bonnet?'
Witchy kitchy kitchy wee,
Spikky wikky mikky bee,
Chippy wippy chee!

V

" Let us both fly up to town:
There I'll buy you such a gown!
[148]

Which, completely in the fashion,
You shall tie a sky-blue sash on;
And a pair of slippers neat
To fit your darling little feet,
So that you will look and feel
Quite galloobious and genteel.
  Jikky wikky bikky see,
  Chicky bikky wikky bee,
   Twicky witchy wee!"

VI

So they both to London went,
Alighting on the Monument;
Whence they flew down swiftly—pop!
Into Moses' wholesale shop:
There they bought a hat and bonnet,
And a gown with spots upon it,
A satin sash of Cloxam blue,
And a pair of slippers too.
  Zikky wikky mikky bee,
  Witchy witchy mitchy kee,
   Sikky tikky wee!

VII

Then, when so completely dressed,
Back they flew, and reached their nest.

Their children cried, " O ma and pa!
How truly beautiful you are! "
Said they, " We trust that cold or pain
We shall never feel again;
While, perched on tree or house or steeple,
We now shall look like other people.
    Withcy witchy witchy wee,
    Twikky mikky bikky bee,
     Zikky sikky tee! "

THE BROOM, THE SHOVEL, THE POKER AND THE TONGS

I

THE Broom and the Shovel, the Poker and Tongs,
    They all took a drive in the Park;
And they each sang a song, ding-a-dong, ding-a-dong!
    Before they went back in the dark.
Mr. Poker he sate quite upright in the coach;
    Mr. Tongs made a clatter and clash;
Miss Shovel was dressed all in black (with a brooch);
    Mrs. Broom was in blue (with a sash).
      Ding-a-dong, ding-a-dong!
      And they all sang a song.

[145]

II

" O Shovely so lovely! " the Poker he sang,
    " You have perfectly conquered my heart.
Ding-a-dong, ding-a-dong! If you're pleased with my song,
    I will feed you with cold apple-tart.
When you scrape up the coals with a delicate sound,
    You enrapture my life with delight,
Your nose is so shiny, your head is so round,
    And your shape is so slender and bright!
        Ding-a-dong, ding-a-dong!
        Ain't you pleased with my song? "

III

" Alas! Mrs. Broom," sighed the Tongs in his song,
    " Oh! is it because I'm so thin,
And my legs are so long,—ding-a-dong, ding-a-dong!—
    That you don't care about me a pin?
Ah! fairest of creatures, when sweeping the room,
    Ah! why don't you heed my complaint?
Must you needs be so cruel, you beautiful Broom,
    Because you are covered with paint?
        Ding-a-dong, ding-a-dong!
        You are certainly wrong."

IV

Mrs. Broom and Miss Shovel together they sang,
  "What nonsense you 're singing to-day!"
Said the Shovel, " I 'll certainly hit you a bang! "
  Said the Broom, " And I 'll sweep you away! "
So the coachman drove homeward as fast as he could,
  Perceiving their anger with pain;
But they put on the kettle, and little by little
  They all became happy again.
      Ding-a-dong, ding-a-dong!
      There's an end of my song.

THE TABLE AND THE CHAIR

I

SAID the Table to the Chair,
  " You can hardly be aware
How I suffer from the heat
And from chilblains on my feet.
If we took a little walk,
We might have a little talk;
Pray let us take the air,"
Said the Table to the Chair.

II

Said the Chair unto the Table,
"Now, you *know* we are not able:
How foolishly you talk,

[147]

When you know we *cannot* walk!",
Said the Table with a sigh,
"It can do no harm to try.
I've as many legs as you:
Why can't we walk on two?"

III

So they both went slowly down,
And walked about the town
With a cheerful bumpy sound
As they toddled round and round;
And everybody cried,
As they hastened to their side,
" See! the Table and the Chair
Have come out to take the air!"

IV

But in going down an alley,
To a castle in a valley,
They completely lost their way,
And wandered all the day;
Till, to see them safely back,
They paid a Ducky-quack,
And a Beetle, and a Mouse,
Who took them to their house.

V

Then they whispered to each other,
"·O delightful little brother,
What a lovely walk we've taken!
Let us dine on beans and bacon."
So the Ducky and the leetle
Browny-Mousy and the Beetle

Dined, and danced upon their heads
Till they toddled to their beds.

THE STORY OF THE FOUR LITTLE CHILDREN
WHO WENT AROUND THE WORLD

ONCE upon a time, a long while ago, there were four little
people whose names were

VIOLET,   SLINGSBY,   GUY, and   LIONEL;
and they all thought they should like to see the world. So they
bought a large boat to sail quite round the world by sea, and
then they were to come back on the other side by land. The
boat was painted blue with green spots, and the sail was yellow
with red stripes: and, when they set off, they only took a small

Cat to steer and look after the boat, besides an elderly Quangle-Wangle, who had to cook the dinner and make the tea; for which purposes they took a large kettle.

For the first ten days they sailed on beautifully, and found plenty to eat, as there were lots of fish; and they had only to take them out of the sea with a long spoon, when the Quangle-Wangle instantly cooked them; and the Pussy-Cat was fed with the bones, with which she expressed herself pleased, on the whole: so that all the party were very happy.

During the daytime, Violet chiefly occupied herself in putting salt water into a churn; while her three brothers churned it violently, in the hope that it would turn into butter, which it seldom if ever did; and in the evening they all retired into the tea-kettle, where they all managed to sleep very comfortably, while Pussy and the Quangle-Wangle managed the boat.

After a time, they saw some land at a distance; and, when they came to it, they found it was an island made of water quite surrounded by earth. Besides that, it was bordered by evanescent isthmuses, with a great gulf-stream running about all over it; so that it was perfectly beautiful, and contained only a single tree, 503 feet high.

When they had landed, they walked about, but found, to their great surprise, that the island was quite full of veal-cutlets and chocolate-drops, and nothing else. So they all climbed up the single high tree to discover, if possible, if there were any people; but having remained on the top of the tree for a week, and not seeing anybody, they naturally concluded that there were no inhabitants; and accordingly, when they came down, they loaded the boat with two thousand veal-cutlets and a million of chocolate-drops; and these afforded them sustenance for

more than a month, during which time they pursued their voyage with the utmost delight and apathy.

After this they came to a shore where there were no less than sixty-five great red parrots with blue tails, sitting on a rail all of a row, and all fast asleep. And I am sorry to say that the Pussy-Cat and the Quangle-Wangle crept softly, and bit off the tail-feathers of all the sixty-five parrots; for which Violet reproved them both severely.

Notwithstanding which, she proceeded to insert all the feathers—two hundred and sixty in number—in her bonnet; thereby causing it to have a lovely and glittering appearance; highly prepossessing and efficacious.

The next thing that happened to them was in a narrow part of the sea, which was so entirely full of fishes that the boat could go on no farther: so they remained there about six weeks, till they had eaten nearly all the fishes, which were soles, and all ready-cooked, and covered with shrimp-sauce, so that there was no trouble whatever. And as the few fishes who remained uneaten complained of the cold, as well as of the difficulty they

had in getting any sleep on account of the extreme noise made by the arctic bears and the tropical turnspits, which frequented

the neighbourhood in great numbers, Violet most amiably knitted a small woollen frock for several of the fishes, and Slingsby administered some opium-drops to them; through which kindness they became quite warm, and slept soundly.

Then they came to a country which was wholly covered with immense orange-trees of a vast size, and quite full of fruit. So they all landed, taking with them the tea-kettle, intending to gather some of the oranges, and place them in it. But, while they were busy about this, a most dreadfully high wind

rose, and blew out most of the parrot-tail feathers from Violet's bonnet. That, however, was nothing compared with the calamity of the oranges falling down on their heads by millions and millions, which thumped and bumped and bumped and thumped them all so seriously, that they were obliged to run as hard as they could for their lives; besides that the sound of the oranges rattling on the tea-kettle was of the most fearful and amazing nature.

Nevertheless, they got safely to the boat, although considerably vexed and hurt; and the Quangle-Wangle's right foot was so knocked about, that he had to sit with his head in his slipper for at least a week.

This event made them all for a time rather melancholy: and perhaps they might never have become less so, had not Lionel, with a most praiseworthy devotion and perseverance, continued to stand on one leg, and whistle to them in a loud and

lively manner; which diverted the whole party so extremely that they gradually recovered their spirits, and agreed that

whenever they should reach home, they would subscribe towards a testimonial to Lionel, entirely made of gingerbread
and raspberries, as an earnest token of their sincere and grateful infection.

After sailing on calmly for several more days, they came
to another country, where they were much pleased and sur-
prised to see a countless multitude of white Mice with red eyes,
all sitting in a great circle, slowly eating custard-pudding with
the most satisfactory and polite demeanour.

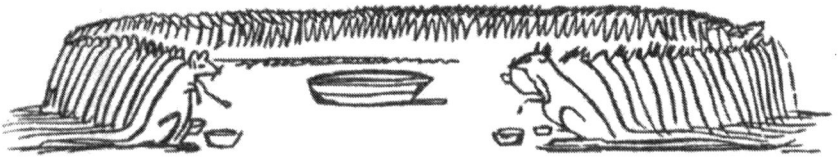

And as the four travellers were rather hungry, being tired
of eating nothing but soles and oranges for so long a period,
they held a council as to the propriety of asking the Mice for
some of their pudding in a humble and affecting manner, by
which they could hardly be otherwise than gratified. It was
agreed, therefore, that Guy should go and ask the Mice, which
he immediately did; and the result was, that they gave a walnut-
shell only half full of custard diluted with water. Now, this
displeased Guy, who said, " Out of such a lot of pudding as you

have got, I must say, you might have spared a somewhat larger
quantity." But no sooner had he finished speaking than the

Mice turned round at once, and sneezed at him in an appalling and vindictive manner (and it is impossible to imagine a more scroobious and unpleasant sound than that caused by the simultaneous sneezing of many millions of angry Mice); so that Guy rushed back to the boat, having first shied his cap into the middle of the custard-pudding, by which means he completely spoiled the Mice's dinner.

By and by the four children came to a country where there were no houses, but only an incredibly innumerable number of large bottles without corks, and of a dazzling and sweetly susceptible blue colour. Each of these blue bottles contained a Blue-Bottle-Fly; and all these interesting animals live continually together in the most copious and rural harmony: nor perhaps in many parts of the world is such perfect and abject happiness to be found. Violet and Slingsby and Guy and Lionel were greatly struck with this singular and instructive settlement; and, having previously asked permission of the Blue-Bottle-Flies (which was most courteously granted), the boat was drawn up to the shore, and they proceeded to make tea in front of the bottles: but as they had no tea-leaves, they

merely placed some pebbles in the hot water; and the Quangle-Wangle played some tunes over it on an accordion, by which, of course, tea was made directly, and of the very best quality.

The four children then entered into conversation with the Blue-Bottle-Flies, who discoursed in a placid and genteel manner, though with a slightly buzzing accent, chiefly owing to the fact that they each held a small clothes-brush between their teeth, which naturally occasioned a fizzy, extraneous utterance.

"Why," said Violet, " would you kindly inform us, do you reside in bottles; and, if in bottles at all, why not, rather, in green or purple, or, indeed, in yellow bottles?"

To which questions a very aged Blue-Bottle-Fly answered, " We found the bottles here all ready to live in; that is to say, our great-great-great-great-great-grandfathers did: so we occupied them at once. And, when the winter comes on, we turn the bottles upside down, and consequently rarely feel the cold at all; and you know very well that this could not be the case with bottles of any other colour than blue."

"Of course it could not," said Slingsby. "But, if we may take the liberty of inquiring, on what do you chiefly subsist?"

"Mainly on oyster-patties," said the Blue-Bottle-Fly; " and, when these are scarce, on raspberry vinegar and Russian leather boiled down to a jelly."

"How delicious!" said Guy.

To which Lionel added, "Huzz!" And all the Blue-Bottle-Flies said, "Buzz!"

At this time, an elderly Fly said it was the hour for the evening-song to be sung; and, on a signal being given, all the Blue-Bottle-Flies began to buzz at once in a sumptuous and sonorous manner, the melodious and mucilaginous sounds echoing all over the waters, and resounding across the tumultuous tops of the transitory titmice upon the intervening and verdant mountains with a serene and sickly suavity only known to the truly virtuous. The Moon was shining slobaciously from the star-bespangled sky, while her light irrigated the smooth and shiny sides and wings and backs of the Blue-Bottle-Flies with

a peculiar and trivial splendour, while all Nature cheerfully re-
sponded to the cerulean and conspicuous circumstances.

In many long-after years, the four little travellers looked
back to that evening as one of the happiest in all their lives; and
it was already past midnight when—the sail of the boat having
been set up by the Quangle-Wangle, the tea-kettle and churn
placed in their respective positions, and the Pussy-Cat stationed
at the helm—the children each took a last and affectionate farewell of the Blue-Bottle-Flies, who walked down in a body to
the water's edge to see the travellers embark.

As a token of parting respect and esteem, Violet made a
courtesy quite down to the ground, and stuck one of her few re-

maining parrot-tail feathers into the back hair of the most
pleasing of the Blue-Bottle-Flies; while Slingsby, Guy, and
Lionel offered them three small boxes, containing, respectively,
black pins, dried figs, and Epsom salts; and thus they left that
happy shore forever.

Overcome by their feelings, the four little travellers instantly jumped into the tea-kettle, and fell fast asleep. But
all along the shore, for many hours, there was distinctly heard
a sound of severely-suppressed sobs, and of a vague multitude
of living creatures using their pocket-handkerchiefs in a sub-

dued simultaneous snuffle, lingering sadly along the walloping waves as the boat sailed farther and farther away from the Land of the Happy Blue-Bottle-Flies.

Nothing particular occurred for some days after these events, except that, as the travellers were passing a low tract of sand, they perceived an unusual and gratifying spectacle; namely, a large number of Crabs and Crawfish—perhaps six or seven hundred—sitting by the water-side, and endeavouring to disentangle a vast heap of pale pink worsted, which they moistened at intervals with a fluid composed of lavender-water and white-wine negus.

" Can we be of any service to you, O crusty Crabbies? " said the four children.

" Thank you kindly," said the Crabs consecutively. " We are trying to make some worsted mittens, but do not know how."

On which Violet, who was perfectly acquainted with the art of mitten-making, said to the Crabs, " Do your claws un-screw, or are they fixtures? "

" They are all made to unscrew," said the Crabs; and forthwith they deposited a great pile of claws close to the boat, with which Violet uncombed all the pale pink worsted, and then made the loveliest mittens with it you can imagine. These the Crabs, having resumed and screwed on their claws, placed cheerfully upon their wrists, and walked away rapidly on their hind-legs, warbling songs with a silvery voice and in a minor key.

After this, the four little people sailed on again till they came to a vast and wide plain of astonishing dimensions, on which nothing whatever could be discovered at first; but, as the travellers walked onward, there appeared in the extreme and dim distance a single object, which on a nearer approach, and on an accurately cutaneous inspection seemed to be somebody

·in a large white wig, sitting on an arm-chair made of sponge-cakes and oyster-shells. " It does not quite look like a human being," said Violet doubtfully; nor could they make out what it really was, till the Quangle-Wangle (who had previously been round the world) exclaimed softly in a loud voice, "It is the co-operative Cauliflower! "

And so, in truth, it was: and they soon found that what they had taken for an immense wig was in reality the top of the Cauliflower; and that he had no feet at all, being able to walk tolerably well with a fluctuating and graceful movement on a single cabbage-stalk,—an accomplishment which naturally saved him the expense of stockings and shoes.

Presently, while the whole party from the boat was gazing at him with mingled affection and disgust, he suddenly arose,

and, in a somewhat plumdomphious manner, hurried off towards the setting sun,—his steps supported by two superincumbent confidential Cucumbers, and a large number of Water-wagtails proceeding in advance of him by three and three in a row,—till he finally disappeared on the brink of the western sky in a crystal cloud of sudorific sand.

So remarkable a sight, of course, impressed the four children very deeply; and they returned immediately to their boat with a strong sense of undeveloped asthma and a great appetite.

Shortly after this, the travellers were obliged to sail directly below some high overhanging rocks, from the top of one of which a particularly odious little boy, dressed in rose-coloured knickerbockers, and with a pewter plate upon his head, threw an enormous pumpkin at the boat, by which it was instantly upset.

But this upsetting was of no consequence, because all the partly knew how to swim very well: and, in fact, they preferred swimming about till after the moon rose; when, the water growing chilly, they sponge-taneously entered the boat. Meanwhile the Quangle-Wangle threw back the pumpkin with immense force, so that it hit the rocks where the malicious little boy in rose-coloured knickerbockers was sitting; when, being quite full f lucifer-matches, the pumpkin exploded surreptitiously into thousand bits; whereon the rocks instantly took fire, and the dious little boy became unpleasantly hotter and hotter and otter, till his knickerbockers were turned quite green, and is nose was burnt off.

Two or three days after this had happened, they came to nother place, where they found nothing at all except some vide and deep pits full of mulberry-jam. This is the property f the tiny, yellow-nosed Apes who abound in these districts, nd who store up the mulberry-jam for their food in winter, hen they mix it with pellucid pale periwinkle-soup, and serve t out in wedgewood china-bowls, which grow freely all over hat part of the country. Only one of the yellow-nosed Apes vas on the spot, and he was fast asleep; yet the four travellers nd the Quangle-Wangle and Pussy were so terrified by the iolence and sanguinary sound of his snoring, that they merely ook a small cupful of the jam, and returned to re-embark in heir boat without delay.

What was their horror on seeing the boat (including the hurn and the tea-kettle) in the mouth of an enormous Seeze

yder, an aquatic and ferocious creature truly dreadful to be-old, and, happily, only met with in those excessive longitudes! n a moment, the beautiful boat was bitten into fifty-five thou-and million hundred billion bits; and it instantly became quite clear that Violet, Slingsby, Guy, and Lionel could no longer preliminate their voyage by sea.

The four travellers were therefore obliged to resolve on pursuing their wanderings by land: and, very fortunately, there happened to pass by at that moment an elderly Rhinoceros, on which they seized; and, all four mounting on his back,—the Quangle-Wangle sitting on his horn, and holding on by his

ears, and the Pussy-Cat swinging at the end of his tail,—they set off, having only four small beans and three pounds of mashed potatoes to last through their whole journey.

They were, however, able to catch numbers of the chickens and turkeys and other birds who incessantly alighted on the head of the Rhinoceros for the purpose of gathering the seeds of the rhododendron-plants which grew there; and these creatures they cooked in the most translucent and satisfactory manner by means of a fire lighted on the end of the Rhinoceros's back. A crowd of Kangaroos and gigantic Cranes accompanied them, from feelings of curiosity and complacency; so that they were never at a loss for company, and went onward, as it were, in a sort of profuse and triumphant procession.

Thus in less than eighteen weeks they all arrived safely at

home, where they were received by their admiring relatives with joy tempered with contempt, and where they finally resolved to carry out the rest of their travelling-plans at some more favourable opportunity.

As for the Rhinoceros, in token of their grateful adherence, they had him killed and stuffed directly, and then set him up outside the door of their father's house as a diaphanous doorscraper.

THE HISTORY OF THE SEVEN FAMILIES OF THE LAKE PIPPLE-POPPLE

CHAPTER I

I N former days,—that is to say, once upon a time,—there lived in the Land of Gramble-Blamble seven families. They lived by the side of the great Lake Pipple-Popple (one of the seven families, indeed, lived *in* the lake), and on the outskirts of the city of Tosh, which, excepting when it was quite dark, they could see plainly. The names of all these places you have probably heard of; and you have only not to look in your geography-books to find out all about them.

Now, the seven families who lived on the borders of the great Lake Pipple-Popple were as follows in the next chapter.

CHAPTER II

THERE was a family of two old Parrots and seven young Parrots.

There was a family of two old Storks and seven young storks.

There was a family of two old Geese and seven young Geese.

There was a family of two old Owls and seven young Owls.

There was a family of two old Guinea Pigs and seven young Guinea Pigs.

There was a family of two old Cats and seven young Cats.

And there was a family of two old Fishes and seven young Fishes.

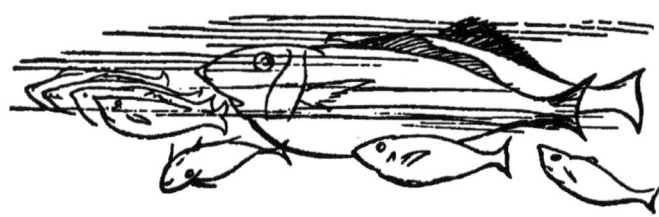

CHAPTER III

THE Parrots lived upon the Soffsky-Poffsky trees, which were beautiful to behold, and covered with blue leaves; and they fed upon fruit, artichokes, and striped beetles.

The Storks walked in and out of the Lake Pipple-Popple, and ate frogs for breakfast, and buttered toast for tea; but on account of the extreme length of their legs they could not sit down, and so they walked about continually.

The Geese, having webs to their feet, caught quantities of flies, which they ate for dinner.

The Owls anxiously looked after mice, which they caught, and made into sago-puddings.

The Guinea Pigs toddled about the gardens, and ate lettuces and Cheshire cheese.

The Cats sate still in the sunshine, and fed upon sponge biscuits.

The Fishes lived in the lake, and fed chiefly on boiled periwinkles.

And all these seven families lived together in the utmost fun and felicity.

CHAPTER IV

ONE day all the seven fathers and the seven mothers of the seven families agreed that they would send their children out to see the world.

So they called them all together, and gave them each eight shillings and some good advice, some chocolate-drops, and a small green morocco pocket-book to set down their expenses in.

They then particularly entreated them not to quarrel; and all the parents sent off their children with a parting injunction.

" If," said the old Parrots, " you find a cherry, do not fight about who should have it."

" And," said the old Storks, " if you find a frog, divide it carefully into seven bits, but on no account quarrel about it."

And the old Geese said to the seven young Geese, " Whatever you do, be sure you do not touch a plum-pudding flea."

And the old Owls said, " If you find a mouse, tear him up into seven slices, and eat him cheerfully, but without quarrelling."

And the old Guinea Pigs said, " Have a care that you eat your lettuces, should you find any, not greedily, but calmly."

And the old Cats said, " Be particularly careful not to meddle with a clangle-wangle if you should see one."

And the old Fishes said, " Above all things, avoid eating

a blue boss-woss; for they do not agree with fishes, and give them a pain in their toes."

So all the children of each family thanked their parents; and, making in all forty-nine polite bows, they went into the wide world.

CHAPTER V

THE seven young Parrots had not gone far, when they saw a tree with a single cherry on it, which the oldest Parrot picked instantly; but the other six, being extremely hungry, tried to get it also. On which all the seven began to fight; and they scuffled,

and huffled,

and ruffled,

and shuffled,

and puffled,

and muffled,

and buffled,

and duffled,

and fluffled,

and guffled,

and bruffled,

and screamed, and shrieked and squealed, and squeaked, and clawed, and snapped, and bit, and bumped, and thumped, and dumped, and flumped each other, till they were all torn into little bits; and at last there was nothing left to record this painful incident except the cherry and seven small green feathers.

And that was the vicious and voluble end of the seven young Parrots.

CHAPTER VI

WHEN the seven young Storks set out, they walked or flew for fourteen weeks in a straight line, and for six weeks more in a crooked one; and after that they ran as hard as they could for one hundred and eight miles; and after that they stood still, and made a himmeltanious chatter-clatter-blattery noise with their bills.

About the same time they perceived a large frog, spotted with green, and with a sky-blue stripe under each ear.

So, being hungry, they immediately flew at him, and were going to divide him into seven pieces, when they began to quarrel as to which of his legs should be taken off first. One said this, and another said that; and while they were all quarrelling, the frog hopped away. And when they saw that he was gone, they began to chatter-clatter,

blatter-platter,

patter-blatter,

matter-clatter,

flatter-quatter, more violently than ever; and after they had fought for a week, they pecked each other all to little pieces, so that at last nothing was left of any of them except their bills.

[178]

And that was the end of the seven young Storks.

CHAPTER VII

WHEN the seven young Geese began to travel, they went over a large plain, on which there was but one tree, and that was a very bad one.

So four of them went up to the top of it, and looked about them; while the other three waddled up and down, and repeated poetry, and their last six lessons in arithmetic, geography, and cookery.

Presently they perceived, a long way off, an object of the most interesting and obese appearance, having a perfectly round body exactly resembling a boiled plum-pudding, with two little wings, and a beak, and three feathers growing out of his head, and only one leg.

So, after a time, all the seven young Geese said to each other, "Beyond all doubt this beast must be a Plum-pudding Flea!"

On which they incautiously began to sing aloud,

> "Plum-pudding Flea,
> Plum-pudding Flea,
> Wherever you be,
> Oh! come to our tree,
> And listen, oh! listen, oh! listen to me!"

And no sooner had they sung this verse than the Plum-pudding Flea began to hop and skip on his one leg with the most dreadful velocity, and came straight to the tree, where he stopped, and looked about him in a vacant and voluminous manner.

[180]

On which the seven young Geese were greatly alarmed, and all of a tremble-bemble: so one of them put out his long neck, and just touched him with the tip of his bill; but no sooner had he done this than the Plum-pudding Flea skipped and hopped about more and more, and higher and higher; after which he opened his mouth, and, to the great surprise and indignation of the seven Geese, began to bark so loudly and furiously and terribly, that they were totally unable to bear the noise; and by degrees every one of them suddenly tumbled down quite dead.

So that was the end of the seven young Geese.

CHAPTER VIII

THE HISTORY OF THE SEVEN YOUNG OWLS

WHEN the seven young Owls set out, they sate every now and then on the branches of old trees, and never went far at one time.

And one night, when it was quite dark, they thought they heard a mouse; but, as the gas-lamps were not lighted, they could not see him.

So they called out, " Is that a mouse? "

On which a mouse answered, "Squeaky-peeky-weeky! yes, it is! "

And immediately all the young Owls threw themselves off the tree, meaning to alight on the ground; but they did not perceive that there was a large well below them, into which they all fell superficially, and were every one of them drowned in less than half a minute.

So that was the end of the seven young Owls.

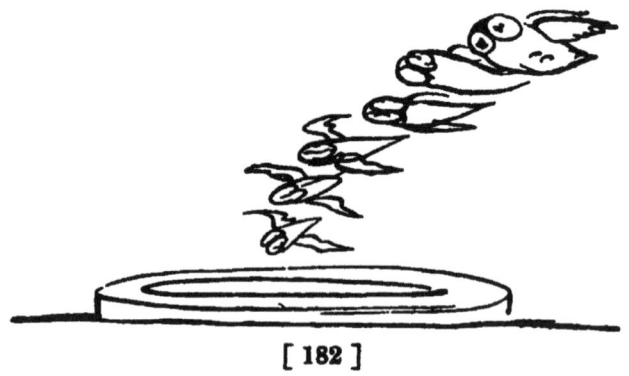

CHAPTER IX

THE seven young Guinea Pigs went into a garden full of gooseberry-bushes and tiggory-trees, under one of which they fell asleep. When they awoke, they saw a large lettuce, which had grown out of the ground while they had been sleeping, and which had an immense number of green leaves. At which they all exclaimed,—

> "Lettuce! O lettuce
> Let us, O let us,
> O lettuce-leaves,
> O let us leave this tree, and eat
> Lettuce, O let us, lettuce-leaves!"

And instantly the seven young Guinea Pigs rushed with such extreme force against the lettuce-plant, and hit their heads so vividly against its stalk, that the concussion brought on directly an incipient transitional inflammation of their noses, which grew worse and worse and worse and worse, till it incidentally killed them all seven.

And that was the end of the seven young Guinea Pigs.

CHAPTER X

THE HISTORY OF THE SEVEN YOUNG CATS

THE seven young Cats set off on their travels with great delight and rapacity. But, on coming to the top of a high hill, they perceived at a long distance off a Clangle-Wangle (or, as it is more properly written, Clangel-Wangel); and, in spite of the warning they had had, they ran straight up to it.

(Now, the Clangle-Wangle is a most dangerous and delusive beast, and by no means commonly to be met with. They live in the water as well as on land, using their long tail as a sail when in the former element. Their speed is extreme; but their habits of life are domestic and superfluous, and their general demeanour pensive and pellucid. On summer evenings, they may sometimes be observed near the Lake Pipple-Popple, standing on their heads, and humming their national melodies. They subsist entirely on vegetables, excepting when they eat veal or mutton or pork or beef or fish or saltpetre.)

The moment the Clangle-Wangle saw the seven young Cats approach, he ran away; and as he ran straight on for four months, and the Cats, though they continued to run, could never overtake him, they all gradually *died* of fatigue and exhaustion, and never afterwards recovered.

And this was the end of the seven young Cats.

CHAPTER XI

THE seven young Fishes swam across the Lake Pipple-Popple, and into the river, and into the ocean; where most unhappily for them, they saw, on the fifteenth day of their travels, a bright-blue Boss-Woss, and instantly swam after him. But the Blue Boss-Woss plunged into a perpendicular,

spicular,

orbicular,

quadrangular,

circular depth of soft mud;

where, in fact, his house was.

And the seven young Fishes, swimming with great and uncomfortable velocity, plunged also into the mud quite against their will, and not being accustomed to it, were all suffocated in a very short period.

And that was the end of the seven young Fishes.

CHAPTER XII

A FTER it was known that the
        seven young Parrots,
   and the seven young Storks,
   and the seven young Geese,
   and the seven young Owls,
   and the seven young Guinea Pigs,
   and the seven young Cats,
   and the seven young Fishes,
were all dead, then the Frog, and the Plum-Pudding Flea, and
the Mouse, and the Clangle-Wangle, and the Blue Boss-Woss,

all met together to rejoice over their good fortune. And they
collected the seven feathers of the seven young Parrots, and
the seven bills of the seven young Storks, and the lettuce, and

the cherry; and having placed the latter on the lettuce, and the other objects in a circular arrangement at their base, they danced a hornpipe round all these memorials until they were quite tired; after which they gave a tea-party, and a garden-party, and a ball, and a concert, and then returned to their respective homes full of joy and respect, sympathy, satisfaction, and disgust.

CHAPTER XIII

OF WHAT BECAME OF THE PARENTS OF THE FORTY-NINE
CHILDREN

BUT when the two old Parrots,
    and the two old Storks,
    and the two old Geese,
    and the two old Owls,
    and the two old Guinea Pigs,
    and the two old Cats,
    and the two old Fishes,
became aware, by reading in the newspapers, of the calamitous
extinction of the whole of their families, they refused all further sustenance; and, sending out to various shops, they purchased great quantities of Cayenne pepper and brandy and
vinegar and blue sealing-wax, besides seven immense glass
bottles with air-tight stoppers. And, having done this, they
ate a light supper of brown-bread and Jerusalem artichokes,
and took an affecting and formal leave of the whole of their
acquaintance, which was very numerous and distinguished and
select and responsible and ridiculous.

CHAPTER XIV

CONCLUSION

AND after this they filled the bottles with the ingredients for pickling, and each couple jumped into a separate bottle; by which effort, of course, they all died immediately, and became thoroughly pickled in a few minutes; having previously made their wills (by the assistance of the most eminent lawyers of the district), in which they left strict orders that the stoppers of the seven bottles should be carefully sealed up with the blue sealing-wax they had purchased; and that they themselves, in the bottles, should be presented to the principal museum of the city of Tosh, to be labelled with parchment or any other anti-congenial succedaneum, and to be placed on a marble table with silver-gilt legs, for the daily inspection and contemplation, and for the perpetual benefit, of the pusillanimous public.

And if you ever happen to go to Gramble-Blamble, and

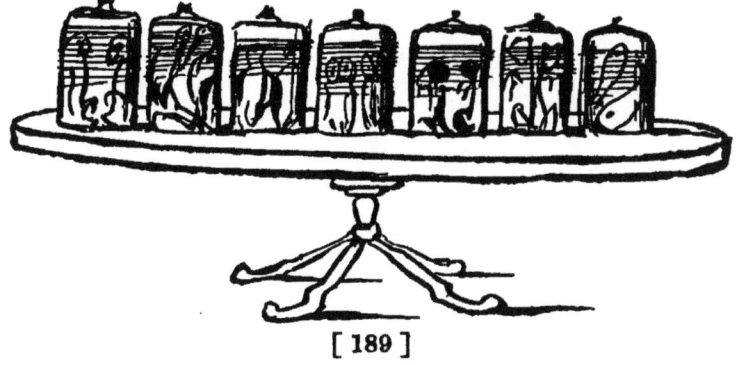

visit that museum in the city of Tosh, look for them on the ninety-eighth table in the four hundred and twenty-seventh room of the right-hand corridor of the left wing of the central quadrangle of that magnificent building; for, if you do not, you certainly will not see them.

NONSENSE COOKERY

NONSENSE COOKERY

Extract from " The Nonsense Gazette," for August, 1870.

OUR readers will be interested in the following com-
munication from our valued and learned contribu-
tor, Prof. Bosh, whose labours in the fields of culinary and botanical science are so well known to all the world.   The first
three articles richly merit to be added to the domestic cookery
of every family: those which follow claim the attention of all
botanists; and we are happy to be able, through Prof. Bosh's
kindness, to present our readers with illustrations of his dis-
coveries.   All the new flowers are found in the Valley of Ver-
rikwier, near the Lake of Oddgrow, and on the summit of the
Hill Orfeltugg."

THREE RECEIPTS FOR DOMESTIC COOKERY

TO MAKE AN AMBLONGUS PIE

TAKE 4 pounds (say 4 1-2 pounds) of fresh Amblongusses, and put them in a small pipkin.

Cover them with water, and boil them for 8 hours incessantly; after which add 2 pints of new milk, and proceed to boil for 4 hours more.

When you have ascertained that the Amblongusses are quite soft, take them out, and place them in a wide pan, taking care to shake them well previously.

Grate some nutmeg over the surface, and cover them carefully with powdered gingerbread, curry-powder, and a sufficient quantity of Cayenne pepper.

Remove the pan into the next room, and place it on the floor. Bring it back again, and let it simmer for three-quarters of an hour. Shake the pan violently till all the Amblongusses have become of a pale purple colour.

Then, having prepared the paste, insert the whole carefully; adding at the same time a small pigeon, 2 slices of beef, 4 cauliflowers, and any number of oysters.

Watch patiently till the crust begins to rise, and add a pinch of salt from time to time.

Serve up in a clean dish, and throw the whole out of window as fast as possible.

TO MAKE CRUMBOBBLIOUS CUTLETS

PROCURE some strips of beef, and, having cut them into the smallest possible slices, proceed to cut them still smaller,—eight, or perhaps nine times.

When the whole is thus minced, brush it up hastily with a new clothes-brush, and stir round rapidly and capriciously with a salt-spoon or a soup-ladle.

Place the whole in a saucepan, and remove it to a sunny place,—say the roof of the house, if free from sparrows or other birds,—and leave it there for about a week.

At the end of that time add a little lavender, some oil of almonds, and a few herring-bones; and then cover the whole with 4 gallons of clarified Crumbobblious sauce, when it will be ready for use.

Cut it into the shape of ordinary cutlets, and serve up in a clean table-cloth or dinner-napkin.

TO MAKE GOSKY PATTIES

TAKE a pig three or four years of age, and tie him by the off hind-leg to a post. Place 5 pounds of currants, 8 of sugar, 2 pecks of peas, 18 roast chestnuts, a candle, and 6 bushels of turnips, within his reach: if he eats these, constantly provide him with more.

Then procure some cream, some slices of Cheshire cheese, 4 quires of foolscap paper, and a packet of black pins. Work the whole into a paste, and spread it out to dry on a sheet of clean brown waterproof linen.

When the paste is perfectly dry, but not before, proceed to beat the pig violently with the handle of a large broom. If he squeals, beat him again.

Visit the paste and beat the pig alternately for some days, and ascertain if, at the end of that period, the whole is about to turn into Gosky Patties.

If it does not then, it never will; and in that case the pig may be let loose, and the whole process may be considered as finished.

NONSENSE BOTANY.

Barkia Howlaloudia.

Enkoopia Chickabiddia.

[199]

Jinglia Tinkettlia.

Nasticreechia Krorfuppia.

Arthbroomia Rigida.

Sophtsluggia Glutinosa.

Minspysia Deliciosa.

Shoebootia Utilis.

Stunnia Dinnerbellia.

Tickia Orologica.

Washtubbia Circularis.

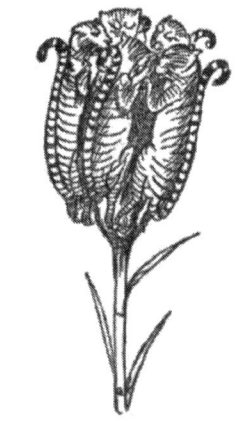

Tigerlillia Terribilis.

NONSENSE BOTANY.

Baccopipia Gracilis.

Bottlephorkia Spoonifolia.

[207]

Cockatooca Superba.

Fishia Marina.

Guittara Pensilis.

Manypeeplia Upsidownia.

Phattfacia Stupenda.

Piggiwiggia Pyramidalis.

Plumbunnia Nutritiosa.

Pollybirdia Singularis.

[211]

NONSENSE BOTANY

Armchairia Comfortabilis.

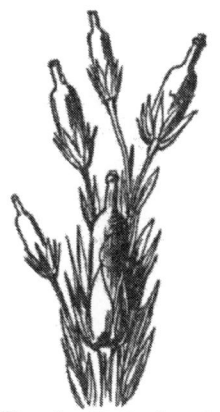

Bassia Palealensis.
[215]

Bubblia Blowpipia.

Bluebottlia Buzztilentia.

Crabbia Horrida.

Smalltoothcombia Domestica.
[217]

Knutmigrata Simplice.

Tureenia Ladlecum.

Puffia Leatherbéllowsa.

Queeriflora Babyöides.
[219]

NONSENSE ALPHABETS

A

A was an ant
Who seldom stood still,
And who made a nice house
In the side of a hill.

a

Nice little ant!

B

B was a book
With a binding of blue,
And pictures and stories
For me and for you.

b

Nice little book!

C

C was a cat
Who ran after a rat;
But his courage did fail
When she seized on his tail.

c

Crafty old cat!

D

D was a duck
With spots on his back,
Who lived in the water,
And always said " Quack!"

d

Dear little duck!

E

E was an elephant,
Stately and wise:
He had tusks and a trunk,
And two queer little eyes.

e

'Oh, what funny small eyes!

F

F was a fish
Who was caught in a net;
But he got out again,
And is quite alive yet.

f

Lively young fish!

G

G was a goat
Who was spotted with brown:
When he did not lie still
He walked up and down.

g

Good little goat!

H

H was a hat
Which was all on one side;
Its crown was too high,
And its brim was too wide.

h

Oh, what a hat!

I

I was some ice
So white and so nice,
But which nobody tasted;
And so it was wasted.

i

'All that good ice!

J

J was a jackdaw
Who hopped up and down
In the principal street
Of a neighbouring town.

j

'All through the town!

K

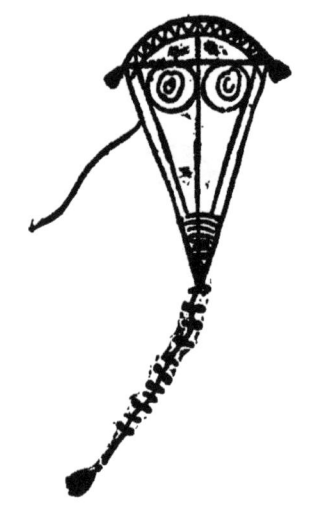

K was a kite
Which flew out of sight,
Above houses so high,
Quite into the sky.

k

Fly away, kite!

L

L was a light
Which burned all the night,
And lighted the gloom
Of a very dark room.

1

Useful nice light!

M

M was a mill
Which stood on a hill,
And turned round and round
With a loud hummy sound.

m
Useful old mill!

N

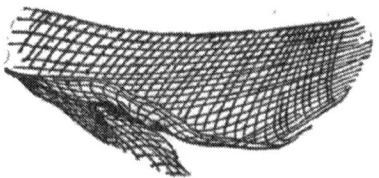

N was a net
Which was thrown in the sea
To catch fish for dinner
For you and for me.

n

Nice little net!

O

O was an orange.
So yellow and round:
When it fell off the tree,
It fell down to the ground.

O

Down to the ground!

P

P was a pig,
Who was not very big;
But his tail was too curly,
And that made him surly.

p

Cross little pig!

Q

Q was a quail
With a very short tail;
And he fed upon corn
In the evening and morn.

q

Quaint little quail!

R

R was a rabbit,
Who had a bad habit
Of eating the flowers
In gardens and bowers.

r

Naughty fat rabbit!

S

S was the sugar-tongs,
Nippity-nee,
To take up the sugar
To put in our tea.

S

Nippity-nee!

T

T was a tortoise,
All yellow and black:
He walked slowly away,
And he never came back.

t

Torty never came back!

U

U was an urn
All polished and bright,
And full of hot water
At noon and at night.

u

Useful old urn!

V

V was a villa
Which stood on a hill,
By the side of a river,
And close to a mill.

V

Nice little villa!

W

W was a whale
With a very long tail,
Whose movements were frantic
Across the Atlantic.

W

Monstrous old whale!

X

X was King Xerxes,
Who, more than all Turks, is
Renowned for his fashion
Of fury and passion.

X
Angry old Xerxes!

Y

Y was a yew,
Which flourished and grew
By a quiet abode
Near the side of a road.

y

Dark little yew!

Z

Z was some zinc,
So shiny and bright,
Which caused you to wink
In the sun's merry light.

Z
Beautiful zinc!

A

a

A was once an apple-pie,
    Pidy,
    Widy,
    Tidy,
    Pidy,
  Nice insidy,
  'Apple-pie!

B

b

B was once a little bear,
    Beary,
    Wary,
    Hairy,
    Beary,
  Taky cary,
  Little bear!

C

c

C was once a little cake,
 Caky,
 Baky,
 Maky,
 Caky,
Taky caky,
Little cake!

D

d

D was once a little doll,
   Dolly,
   Molly,
   Polly,
   Nolly,
   Nursy dolly,
   Little doll!

E

E e

E was once a little eel,
  Eely,
  Weely,
  Peely,
  Eely,
 Twirly, tweely,
  Little eel!

F

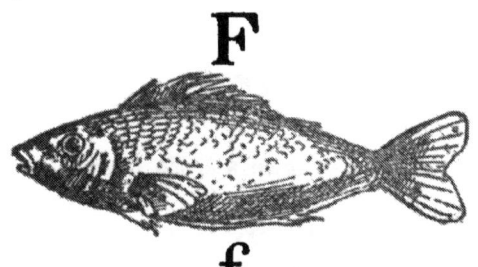

F f

F was once a little fish,
  Fishy,
  Wishy,
  Squishy,
  Fishy,
 In a dishy,
  Little fish!

G

g

G was once a little goose,
    Goosy,
    Moosy,
    Boosey,
    Goosey,
  Waddly-woosy,
  Little goose!

H

h

H was once a little hen,
Henny,
Chenny,
Tenny,
Henny.
Eggsy-any,
Little hen?

I

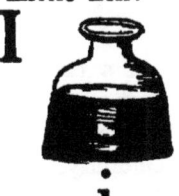

i

I was once a bottle of ink,
Inky,
Dinky,
Thinky,
Inky,
Blacky minky,
Bottle of ink!

[258]

J

j

J was once a jar of jam,
      Jammy,
      Mammy,
      Clammy,
      Jammy,
  Sweety, swammy,
    Jar of jam!

K

k

K was once a little kite,
    Kity,
    Whity,
    Flighty,
    Kity,
  Out of sighty,
  Little kite!

L

l

L was once a little lark,
Larky,
Marky,
Harky,
Larky,
In the parky,
Little lark!

M

m

M was once a little mouse,
Mousy,
Bousy,
Sousy,
Mousy,
In the housy,
Little mouse!

N

n

N was once a little needle,
Needly,
Tweedly,
Threedly,
Needly,
Wisky, wheedly,
Little needle!

O

o

O was once a little owl,
    Owly,
    Prowly,
    Howly,
    Owly,
    Browny fowly,
    Little owl!

P

p

P was once a little pump,
      Pumpy,
      Slumpy,
      Flumpy,
      Pumpy,
   Dumpy, thumpy,
   Little pump!

Q

q

Q was once a little quail,
          Quaily,
          Faily,
          Daily,
          Quaily,
     Stumpy-taily,
     Little quail!

R

r

R was once a little rose,
Rosy,
Posy,
Nosy,
Rosy,
Blows-y, grows-y,
Little rose!

S

S

S was once a little shrimp,
    Shrimpy,
    Nimpy,
    Flimpy,
    Shrimpy.
Jumpy, jimpy,
    Little shrimp!

T

t

T was once a little thrush,
　　　Thrushy,
　　　Hushy,
　　　Bushy,
　　　Thrushy,
　　Flitty, flushy,
　　Little thrush!

U

u

U was once a little urn,
　　Urny,
　　Burny,
　　Turny,
　　Urny,
　Bubbly, burny,
　Little urn!

V

V

V was once a little vine,
    Viny,
    Winy,
    Twiny,
    Viny,
    Twisty-twiny,
    Little vine!

W

W

W was once a whale,
        Whaly,
        Scaly,
        Shaly,
        Whaly,
    Tumbly-taily,
    Mighty whale!

X

X

X was once a great king Xerxes,
Xerxy,
Perxy,
Turxy,
Xerxy,
Linxy, lurxy,
Great King Xerxes!

Y

y

Y was once a little yew,
 Yewdy,
 Fewdy,
 Crudy,
 Yewdy,
Growdy, grewdy,
 Little yew!

Z

Z

Z was once a piece of zinc,
        Tinky,
        Winky,
        Blinky,
        Tinky,
    Tinkly minky,
    Piece of zinc!

A

A was an ape,
Who stole some white tape,
And tied up his toes
In four beautiful bows

a
Funny old ape!

B

B was a bat,
Who slept all the day,
And fluttered about
When the sun went away.

b.

Brown little bat!

C

C was a camel:
　　You rode on his hump;
　　And if you fell off,
　　You came down such a bump!

c

What a high camel!

D

D was a dove,
Who lived in a wood,
With such pretty soft wings,
And so gentle and good!

d

Dear little dove!

E

E was an eagle,
Who sat on the rocks,
And looked down on the fields
And the far-away flocks.

e

Beautiful eagle!

F

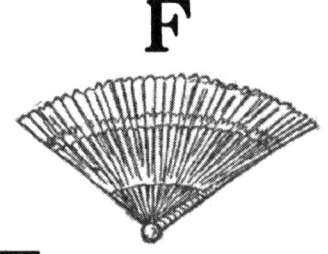

F was a fan
Made of beautiful stuff;
And when it was used,
It went puffy-puff-puff!

f

Nice little fan!

G

G was a gooseberry,
Perfectly red;
To be made into jam,
And eaten with bread.

g

Gooseberry red!

H

H was a heron,
Who stood in a stream:
The length of his neck
And his legs was extreme.

h

Long-legged heron!

I

I was an inkstand,
Which stood on a table,
With a nice pen to write with
When we are able.

i

Neat little inkstand!

J

J was a jug,
So pretty and white,
With fresh water in it
At morning and night.

j

Nice little jug!

K

K was a kingfisher:
Quickly he flew,
So bright and so pretty!—
Green, purple, and blue.

k

Kingfisher blue!

L

L was a lily,
So white and so sweet!
To see it and smell it
Was quite a nice treat.

l

Beautiful lily!

M

M was a man,
Who walked round and round;
And he wore a long coat
That came down to the ground.

m

Funny old man!

N

N was a nut
So smooth and so brown!
And when it was ripe,
It fell tumble-dum-down.

n
Nice little nut!

O

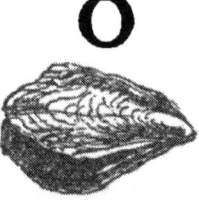

O was an oyster,
Who lived in his shell:
If you let him alone,
He felt perfectly well.

O
Open-mouthed oyster!

[281]

P

P was a polly,
All red, blue, and green,—
The most beautiful polly
That ever was seen.

p

Poor little polly!

Q

Q was a quill
Made into a pen;
But I do not know where,
And I cannot say when.

q

Nice little quill!

R

R was a rattlesnake,
  Rolled up so tight,
  Those who saw him ran quickly,
  For fear he should bite.

r

Rattlesnake bite!

S

S was a screw
  To screw down a box;
  And then it was fastened
  Without any locks.

S

Valuable screw!

[288]

T

T was a thimble,
Of silver so bright!
When placed on the finger,
It fitted so tight!

t

Nice little thimble!

U

U was an upper-coat,
Woolly and warm,
To wear over all
In the snow or the storm.

u

What a nice upper-coat!

[284]

V

V was a veil
With a border upon it,
And a ribbon to tie it
All round a pink bonnet.

V

Pretty green veil!

W

W was a watch,
   Where, in letters of gold,
   The hour of the day
   You might always behold.

W
Beautiful watch!

X

X was King Xerxes,
Who wore on his head
A mighty large turban,
Green, yellow, and red.

X

Look at King Xerxes!

Y

Y was a yak,
From the land of Thibet:
Except his white tail,
He was all black as jet.

y

Look at the yak!

Z

Z was a zebra,
All striped white and black;
And if he were tame,
You might ride on his back.

Z

Pretty striped zebra!

ONE HUNDRED NONSENSE PICTURES
AND RHYMES

There was a young person of Bantry,
Who frequently slept in the pantry;
When disturbed by the mice, she appeased them with rice,
That judicious young person of Bantry.

There was an old person of Minety,
Who purchased five hundred and ninety
Large apples and pears, which he threw unawares
At the heads of the people of Minety.

There was an Old Man at a Junction,
Whose feelings were wrung with compunction
When they said, "The Train's gone!" he exclaimed, "How
  forlorn!"
But remained on the rails of the Junction.

There was an old man of Thermopylœ,
Who never did anything properly;
But they said, "If you choose to boil eggs in your shoes,
You shall never remain in Thermopylœ."

There was an old person of Deal,
Who in walking used only his heel;
When they said, "Tell us why?" he made no reply,
That mysterious old person of Deal.

There was an old man on the Humber,
Who dined on a cake of Burnt Umber;
When he said, "It's enough!" they only said, "Stuff!
You amazing old man on the Humber!"

[295]

There was an old man in a barge,
Whose nose was exceedingly large;
But in fishing by night, it supported a light,
Which helped that old man
     in a barge.

There was an old man of Toulouse
Who purchased a new pair of shoes;
When they asked, "Are they pleasant?" he said, "Not at
    present!"
That turbid old man of Toulouse.

There was an old man of Dunrose;
A parrot seized hold of his nose.
When he grew melancholy, they said, " His name's Polly,"
Which soothed that old man of Dunrose.

There was an old person of Bree,
Who frequented the depths of the sea;
She nurs'd the small fishes, and washed all the dishes,
And swam back again into Bree.

[297]

There was an old person of Shields,
Who frequented the vallies and fields;
All the mice and the cats, and the snakes and the rats,
Followed after that person of Shields.

There was an old person of Bromley,
Whose ways were not cheerful or comely;
He sate in the dust, eating spiders and crust,
That unpleasing old person of Bromley.

There was an old man of Dunluce,
Who went out to sea on a goose:
When he'd gone out a mile, he observ'd with a smile,
" It is time to return to Dunluce."

There was an old man of Dee-side
Whose hat was exceedingly wide,
But he said, " Do not fail, if it happen to hail,
To come under my hat at Dee-side!"

[299]

There was an old person in black,
A Grasshopper jumped on his back;
When it chirped in his ear, he was smitten with fear,
That helpless old person in black.

There was an old man of the Dargle
Who purchased six barrels of Gargle;
For he said, " I'll sit still, and will roll them down hill,
For the fish in the depths of the Dargle."

[300]

There was an old person of Pinner,
As thin as a lath, if not thinner;
They dressed him in white, and roll'd him up tight,
That elastic old person of Pinner.

There was an old man in a Marsh,
Whose manners were futile and harsh;
He sate on a log, and sang songs to a frog,
That instructive old man in a Marsh.

[301]

There was an old person of China,
Whose daughters were Jiska and Dinah,
Amelia and Fluffy, Olivia and Chuffy,
And all of them settled in China.

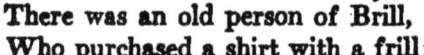

There was an old person of Brill,
Who purchased a shirt with a frill;
But they said, " Don't you wish, you mayn't look like a fish,
You obsequious old person of Brill? "

There was an old man at a Station,
Who made a promiscuous oration;
But they said, "Take some snuff!—You have talk'd quite
    enough,
You afflicting old man at a Station!"

There was an old person of Wick,
Who said, "Tick-a-Tick, Tick-a-Tick;
Chickabee, Chickabaw." And he said nothing more,
That laconic old person of Wick.

[303]

There was an old man of Three Bridges,
Whose mind was distracted by midges,
He sate on a wheel, eating underdone veal,
Which relieved that old man of Three Bridges.

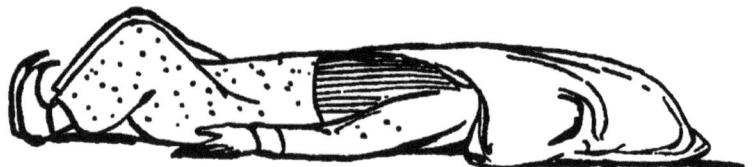

There was an old man of Hong Kong,
Who never did anything wrong;
He lay on his back, with his head in a sack,
That innocuous old man of Hong Kong.

There was an old person of Fife,
Who was greatly disgusted with life;
They sang him a ballad, and fed him on salad,
      Which cured that old person of Fife.

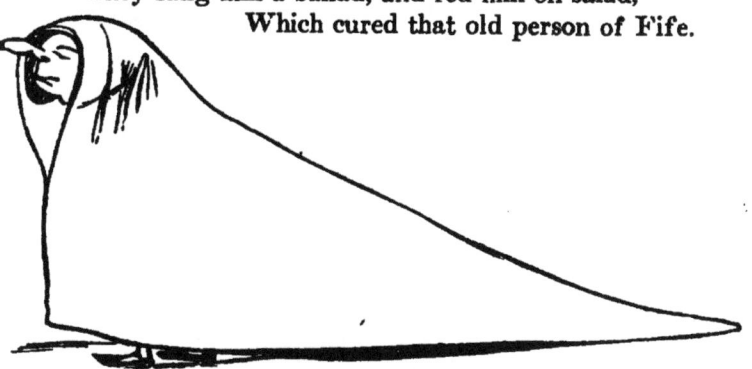

There was a young person in green,
Who seldom was fit to be seen;
She wore a long shawl, over bonnet and all,
Which enveloped that person in green.

There was an old man who screamed out
Whenever they knocked him about:
So they took off his boots, and fed him with fruits,
And continued to knock him about.

There was a young lady in white,
Who looked out at the depths of the night;
But the birds of the air, filled her heart with despair,
And oppressed that young lady in white.

There was an old person of Slough,
Who danced at the end of a bough;
But they said, " If you sneeze, you might damage the trees,
You imprudent old person of Slough."

There was an old person of Down,
Whose face was adorned with a frown;
When he opened the door, for one minute or more,
He alarmed all the people of Down.

[807]

There was a young person in red,
Who carefully covered her head,
With a bonnet of leather, and three lines of feather,
 Besides some long ribands of red.

There was an old person of Hove,
Who frequented the depths of a grove;
Where he studied his books, with the wrens and the rooks,
That tranquil old person of Hove.

There was a young person in pink,
Who called out for something to drink;
But they said, " O my daughter,
 there's nothing but water!"
Which vexed that young person
 in pink.

There was an old lady of France,
Who taught little ducklings to dance;
When she said, " Tick-a-tack!" they only said, " Quack!"
Which grieved that old lady of France.

[309]

There was an old person of Putney,
Whose food was roast spiders and chutney,
Which he took with his tea, within sight of the sea,
That romantic old person of Putney.

There was an old person of Loo,
Who said, "What on earth shall I do?"
When they said, "Go away!" she continued to stay,
That vexatious old person of Loo.

There was an old person of Woking,
Whose mind was perverse and provoking;
He sate on a rail, with his head in a pail,
That illusive old person of Woking.

There was an old person of Dean
Who dined on one pea, and one bean;
For he said, "More than that, would make me too fat."
That cautious old person of Dean.

There was a young lady in blue,
Who said, " Is it you?   Is it you? "
When they said, " Yes, it is," she replied only, " Whizz! "
That ungracious young lady in blue.

There was an old person of Pisa,
Whose daughters did nothing to please her;
She dressed them in grey, and banged them all day,
Round the walls of the city of Pisa.

There was an old man in a garden,
Who always begged every one's pardon;
When they asked him, "What for?" he replied, "You're a
bore!
And I trust you'll go out of my
garden."

There was an old person of Florence,
Who held mutton chops in abhorrence;
He purchased a Bustard, and fried him in Mustard,
Which choked that old person of Florence.

There was an old person of Sheen,
Whose expression was calm and serene;
He sate in the water, and drank bottled porter,
That placid old person of Sheen.

There was an old man of Cashmere,
Whose movements were scroobious and queer;
Being slender and tall, he looked over a wall,
And perceived two fat ducks of Cashmere.

[814]

There was an old person of Ware,
Who rode on the back of a bear:
When they ask'd, "Does it trot?"
    he said, "Certainly not!
He's a Moppsikon Floppsikon bear!"

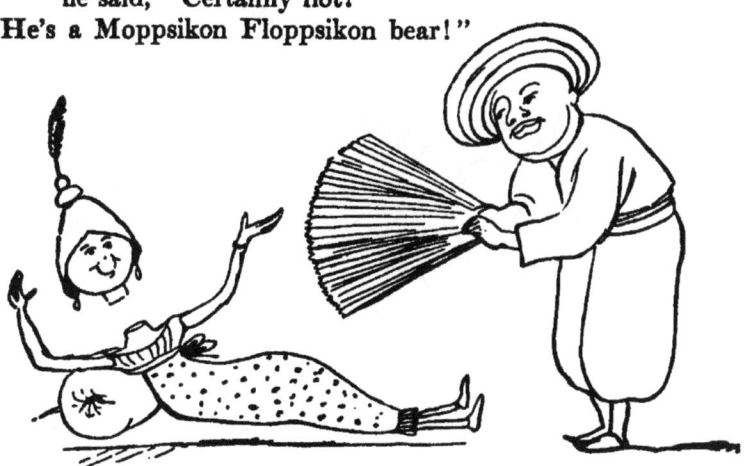

There was a young person of Janina,
Whose uncle was always a fanning her;
When he fanned off her head, she smiled sweetly, and said,
"You propitious old person of Janina!"

There was an old person of Pett,
Who was partly consumed by regret;
He sate in a cart, and ate cold apple tart,
Which relieved that old person of Pett.

There was an old person of Cassel,
Whose nose finished off in a tassel;
But they call'd out, " Oh well! don't it look like a bell! "
Which perplexed that old person of Cassel.

There was an old man of Spithead,
Who opened the window, and said,—
" Fil-jomble, fil-jumble, fil-rumble-come-tumble! "
That doubtful old man of Spithead.

There was an old man on the Border,
Who lived in the utmost disorder;
He danced with the cat, and made tea in his hat,
Which vexed all the folks on the Border.

[317]

There was an old man of Dumbree,
Who taught little owls to drink tea;
For he said, "To eat mice is not proper or nice,"
That amiable man of Dumbree.

There was an old person of Filey,
Of whom his acquaintance spoke highly;
He danced perfectly well, to the sound of a bell,
And delighted the people of Filey.

There was an old man whose remorse
Induced him to drink Caper Sauce;
For they said, " If mixed up with some cold claret-cup,
It will certainly soothe your remorse! "

There was an old man of Ibreem,
Who suddenly threaten'd to scream:
But they said, " If you do, we will thump you quite blue,
You disgusting old man of Ibreem! "

[819]

There was an old person of Wilts,
Who constantly walked upon stilts;
He wreathed them with lilies and daffy-down-dillies,
          That elegant person of Wilts.

There was an old person of Grange,
Whose manners were scroobious and strange;
He sailed to St. Blubb in a waterproof tub,
That aquatic old person of Grange.

There was an old man of Dumblane,
Who greatly resembled a crane;
But they said, " Is it wrong, since your legs are so long,
To request you won't stay in Dumblane?"

There was an old man of El Hums,
Who lived upon nothing but crumbs,
Which he picked off the ground, with the other birds round,
In the roads and the lanes of El Hums.

[321]

There was an old man of West Dumpet,
Who possessed a large nose like a trumpet;
When he blew it aloud, it astonished the crowd,
And was heard through the whole of West Dumpet.

There was an old man of Port Grigor,
Whose actions were noted for vigour;
He stood on his head till his waistcoat turned red,
That eclectic old man of Port Grigor.

[322]

There was an old person of Newry,
Whose manners were tinctured with fury;
He tore all the rugs, and broke all the jugs,
Within twenty miles' distance of Newry.

There was an old person of Sark,
Who made an unpleasant remark;
But they said, " Don't you see what a brute you must be,
You obnoxious old person of Sark! "

There was an old man whose despair
Induced him to purchase a hare:
Whereon one fine day he rode wholly away,
Which partly assuaged his despair.

There was an old person of Barnes,
Whose garments were covered with darns;
But they said, " Without doubt, you will soon wear them out,
You luminous person of Barnes! "

There was an old person of Nice,
Whose associates were usually Geese.
They walked out together in all sorts of weather,
That affable person of Nice!

There was a young lady of Greenwich,
Whose garments were border'd with Spinach;
But a large spotty Calf bit her shawl quite in half,
Which alarmed that young lady of Greenwich.

There was an old person of Cannes,
Who purchased three fowls and a fan;
Those she placed on a stool, and to make them feel cool
She constantly fanned them at Cannes.

There was an old person in grey,
Whose feelings were tinged with dismay;
She purchased two parrots, and fed them with carrots,
Which pleased that old person in grey.

[326]

There was an old person of Hyde,
Who walked by the shore with his bride,
Till a Crab who came near fill'd their bosoms with fear,
And they said, " Would we'd never left Hyde! "

There was an old person of Ickley,
Who could not abide to ride quickly;
He rode to Karnak on a tortoise's back,
That moony old person of Ickley.

[827]

There was an old man of Ancona,
Who found a small dog with no owner,
Which he took up and down all the streets of the town,
That anxious old man of Ancona.

There was an old person of Sestri,
What sate himself down in the vestry;
When they said, " You are wrong! " he merely said " Bong! "
That repulsive old person of Sestri.

There was an old person of Blythe,
Who cut up his meat with a scythe;
When they said, ".Well! I never!" he cried, " Scythes for
    ever!"
That lively old person of Blythe.

There was a young person of Ayr,
Whose head was remarkably square:
On the top, in fine weather, she wore a gold feather;
Which dazzled the people of Ayr.

[329]

There was an old person of Rimini,
Who said, " Gracious! Goodness! O Gimini! "
When they said, " Please be still! " she ran down a hill,
And was never more heard of at Rimini.

There is a young lady, whose nose,
Continually prospers and grows;
When it grew out of sight, she exclaimed in a fright,
" Oh! Farewell to the end of my nose! "

There was an old person of Ealing,
Who was wholly devoid of good feeling;
He drove a small gig, with three Owls and a Pig,
Which distressed all the people of Ealing.

There was an old man of Thames Ditton,
Who called out for something to sit on;
But they brought him a hat, and said, " Sit upon that,
You abruptious old man of Thames Ditton!"

[331]

There was an old person of Bray,
Who sang through the whole of the day
To his ducks and his pigs, whom he fed upon figs,
That valuable person of Bray.

There was a young person whose history
Was always considered a mystery;
She sate in a ditch, although no one knew which,
And composed a small treatise on history.

[882]

There was an old person of Bow,
Whom nobody happened to know;
So they gave him some soap, and said coldly, "We hope
You will go back directly to Bow!"

There was an old person of Rye,
Who went up to town on a fly;
But they said, "If you cough, you are safe to fall off!
You abstemious old person of Rye!"

[888]

There was an old person of Crowle,
Who lived in the nest of an owl;
When they screamed in the nest, he screamed out with the rest,
That depressing old person in Crowle.

There was an old Lady of Winchelsea,
Who said, " If you needle or pin shall see
On the floor of my room, sweep it up with the broom!"
That exhaustive old Lady of Winchelsea!

[384]

There was an old man in a tree,
Whose whiskers were lovely to see;
But the birds of the air pluck'd them perfectly bare,
To make themselves nests in that tree.

There was a young lady of Corsica,
Who purchased a little brown saucy-cur;
Which she fed upon ham, and hot raspberry jam,
That expensive young lady of Corsica.

[335]

There was an old person of Stroud,
Who was horribly jammed in a crowd;
Some she slew with a kick, some she scrunched with a stick,
That impulsive old person of Stroud.

There was a young lady of Firle,
Whose hair was addicted to curl;
It curled up a tree, and all over the sea,
That expansive young lady of Firle.

There was an old man of Boulak,
Who sate on a Crocodile's back;
But they said, " Towr'ds the night he may probably bite,
Which might vex you, old man of Boulak!"

There was an old person of Skye,
Who waltz'd with a Bluebottle fly:
They buzz'd a sweet tune, to the light of the moon,
And entranced all the people of Skye.

[337]

There was an old man of Blackheath,
Whose head was adorned with a wreath
Of lobsters and spice, pickled onions and mice,
That uncommon old man of Blackheath.

There was an old man, who when little,
Fell casually into a kettle;
But growing too stout, he could never get out,
So he passed all his life in that kettle.

There was an old person of Dundalk,
Who tried to teach fishes to walk;
When they tumbled down dead, he grew weary, and said,
" I had better go back to Dundalk!"

There was an old person of Shoreham,
Whose habits were marked by decorum;
He bought an Umbrella, and sate in the cellar,
Which pleased all the people of Shoreham.

There was an old person of Bar,
Who passed all her life in a jar,
Which she painted pea-green, to appear more serene,
That placid old person of Bar.

There was a young person of Kew,
Whose virtues and vices were few;
But with blamable haste she devoured some hot paste,
Which destroyed that young person of Kew.

There was an old person of Jodd,
Whose ways were perplexing and odd;
She purchased a whistle, and sate on a thistle,
And squeaked to the people of Jodd.

There was an old person of Bude,
Whose deportment was vicious and crude;
He wore a large ruff of pale straw-coloured stuff,
Which perplexed all the people of Bude.

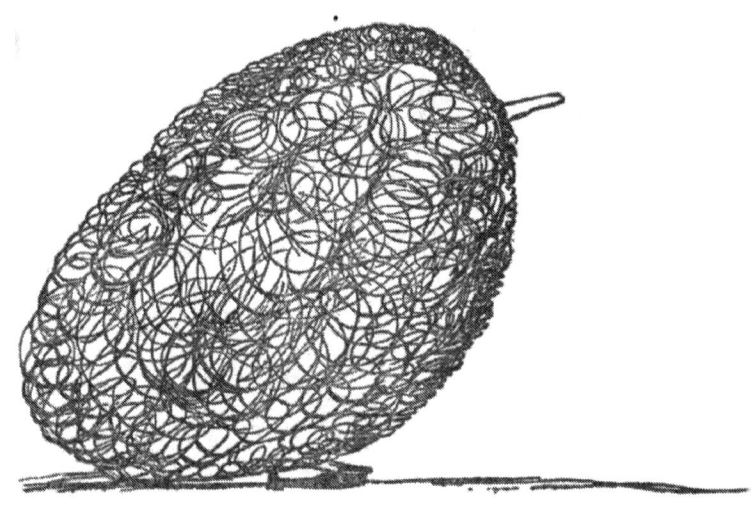

There was an old person of Brigg,
Who purchased no end of a wig;
So that only his nose, and the end of his toes,
Could be seen when he walked about Brigg.

There was an old man of Messina,
Whose daughter was named Opsibeena;
She wore a small wig, and rode out on a pig,
To the perfect delight of Messina.

THE COMPLETE NONSENSE BOOK

AN ALPHABET

The Absolutely Abstemious Ass,
who resided in a Barrel, and only lived on
Soda Water and Pickled Cucumbers.

The Bountiful Beetle,
who always carried a Green Umbrella when it didn't rain,
and left it home when it did.

The Comfortable Confidential Cow,
who sate in her Red Morocco Arm Chair and
toasted her own Bread at the parlour Fire.

The Dolomphious Duck,
who caught Spotted Frogs for her dinner
with a Runcible Spoon.

The Enthusiastic Elephant,
who ferried himself across the water with the
Kitchen Poker and a New pair of Ear-rings.

The Fizzgiggious Fish,
who always walked about upon Stilts,
because he had no legs.

The Good-natured Grey Gull,
who carried the Old Owl, and his Crimson Carpet-bag,
across the river, because he could not swim.

The Hasty Higgeldipiggledy Hen,
who went to market in a Blue Bonnet and Shawl,
and bought a Fish for her Supper.

The Inventive Indian,
who caught a Remarkable Rabbit in a
Stupendous Silver Spoon.

The Judicious Jubilant Jay,
who did up her Back Hair every morning with a Wreath of
     Roses,
Three feathers, and a Gold Pin.

[352]

The Kicking Kangaroo,
who wore a Pale Pink Muslin dress
with Blue spots.

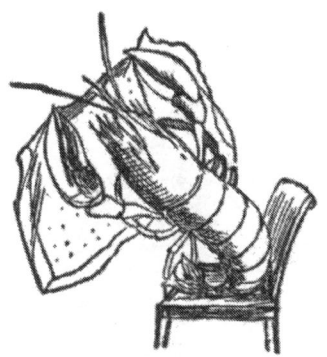

The Lively Learned Lobster,
who mended his own Clothes with
a Needle and Thread.

[358]

The Melodious Meritorious Mouse,
who played a merry minuet on the
Piano-forte.

The Nutritious Newt,
who purchased a Round Plum-pudding
for his grand-daughter.

The Obsequious Ornamental Ostrich,
who wore Boots to keep his
feet quite dry.

The Perpendicular Purple Polly,
who read the Newspaper and ate Parsnip Pie
with his Spectacles.

The Queer Querulous Quail,
who smoked a Pipe of Tobacco on the top of
a Tin Tea-kettle.

The Rural Runcible Raven,
who wore a White Wig and flew away
with the Carpet Broom.

The Scroobious Snake,
who always wore a Hat on his Head, for
fear he should bite anybody.

The Tumultuous Tom-tommy Tortoise,
who beat a Drum all day long in the
middle of the wilderness.

The Umbrageous Umbrella-maker,
whose Face nobody ever saw, because it was
always covered by his Umbrella.

The Visibly Vicious Vulture,
who wrote some Verses to a Veal-cutlet in a
Volume bound in Vellum.

The Worrying Whizzing Wasp,
who stood on a Table, and played sweetly on a
Flute with a Morning Cap.

The Excellent Double-extra XX
imbibing King Xerxes, who lived a
long while ago.

The Yonghy-Bonghy-Bo,
whose Head was ever so much bigger than his
Body, and whose Hat was rather small.

The Zigzag Zealous Zebra,
who carried five monkeys on his back all
the way to Jellibolee.

LAUGHABLE LYRICS

LAUGHABLE LYRICS

THE DONG WITH A LUMINOUS NOSE

WHEN awful darkness and silence reign
 Over the great Gromboolian plain,
  Through the long, long wintry nights;
When the angry breakers roar
As they beat on the rocky shore;
 When Storm-clouds brood on the towering heights
Of the Hills of the Chankly Bore,—

Then, through the vast and gloomy dark
There moves what seems a fiery spark,—
 A lonely spark with silvery rays
  Piercing the coal-black night,—
 A Meteor strange and bright:
Hither and thither the vision strays,
 A single lurid light.

Slowly it wanders, pauses, creeps,—
Anon it sparkles, flashes, and leaps;
And ever as ᴐnward it gleaming goes
A light on the Bong-tree stems it throws.
And those who watch at that midnight hour
From Hall or Terrace or lofty Tower,
Cry, as the wild light passes along,—
    " The Dong! the Dong!
  The wandering Dong through the forest goes!
    The Dong! the Dong!
    The Dong with a luminous Nose! "

    Long years ago
  The Dong was happy and gay,
Till he fell in love with a Jumbly Girl
  Who came to those shores one day.
For the Jumblies came in a sieve, they did,—
Landing at eve near the Zemmery Fidd
    Where the Oblong Oysters grow,
  And the rocks are smooth and grey.
And all the woods and the valleys rang
With the Chorus they daily and nightly sang,—
    " Far and few, far and few,
      Are the lands where the Jumblies live;
      Their heads are green, and their hands are blue,
      And they went to sea in a sieve."

Happily, happily passed those days!
  While the cheerful Jumblies staid;
  They danced in circlets all night long,
  To the plaintive pipe of the lively Dong,
    In moonlight, shine, or shade.
                [364]

For day and night he was always there
By the side of the Jumbly Girl so fair,
With her sky-blue hands and her sea-green hair;
Till the morning came of that hateful day
When the Jumblies sailed in their sieve away,
And the Dong was left on the cruel shore
Gazing, gazing for evermore,—
Ever keeping his weary eyes on
That pea-green sail on the far horizon,—
Singing the Jumbly Chorus still
As he sate all day on the grassy hill,—
> *" Far and few, far and few,*
> *Are the lands where the Jumblies live;*
> *Their heads are green, and their hands are blue,*
> *And they went to sea in a sieve."*

But when the sun was low in the West,
    The Dong arose and said,—
" What little sense I once possessed
    Has quite gone out of my head! "
And since that day he wanders still
By lake and forest, marsh and hill,
Singing, " O somewhere, in valley or plain,
Might I find my Jumbly Girl again!
For ever I'll seek by lake and shore
Till I find my Jumbly Girl once more! "
  Playing a pipe with silvery squeaks,
  Since then his Jumbly Girl he seeks;
  And because by night he could not see,
  He gathered the bark of the Twangum Tree
    On the flowery plain that grows.
    And he wove him a wondrous Nose,—
  A Nose as strange as a Nose could be!

Of vast proportions and painted red,
And tied with cords to the back of his head.
  In a hollow rounded space it ended
  With a luminous lamp within suspended,
    All fenced about
    With a bandage stout
    To prevent the wind from blowing it out;
  And with holes all round to send the light
  In gleaming rays on the dismal night.

And now each night, and all night long,
Over those plains still roams the Dong;
And above the wail of the Chimp and Snipe
You may hear the squeak of his plaintive pipe,
While ever he seeks, but seeks in vain,
To meet with his Jumbly Girl again;
Lonely and wild, all night he goes,—
The Dong with a luminous Nose!
And all who watch at the midnight hour,
From Hall or Terrace or lofty Tower,
Cry, as they trace the Meteor bright,
Moving along through the dreary night,—
  " This is the hour when forth he goes,
  The Dong with a luminous Nose!
  Yonder, over the plain he goes,—
      He goes!
      He goes,—
  The Dong with a luminous Nose!"

THE TWO OLD BACHELORS

TWO old Bachelors were living in one house;
    One caught a Muffin, the other caught a Mouse.
Said he who caught the Muffin to him who caught the Mouse,—
" This happens just in time! For we've nothing in the house,
Save a tiny slice of lemon and a teaspoonful of honey,
And what to do for dinner—since we haven't any money?
And what can we expect if we haven't any dinner,
But to lose our teeth and eyelashes and keep on growing
    thinner?"

Said he who caught the Mouse to him who caught the Muffin,—
" We might cook this little Mouse, if we only had some
    Stuffin' !
If we had but Sage and Onion we could do extremely well;
But how to get that Stuffin' it is difficult to tell!"

Those two old Bachelors ran quickly to the town
And asked for Sage and Onion as they wandered up and down;
They borrowed two large Onions, but no Sage was to be
    found
In the Shops, or in the Market, or in all the Gardens round.

But some one said, " A hill there is, a little to the north,
And to its purpledicular top a narrow way leads forth;
And there among the rugged rocks abides an ancient Sage,—
An earnest Man, who reads all day a most perplexing page.
Climb up, and seize him by the toes,—all studious as he sits,—
And pull him down, and chop him into endless little bits!
Then mix him with your Onion (cut up likewise into Scraps),—
When your Stuffin' will be ready, and very good—perhaps."

Those two old Bachelors without loss of time
The nearly purpledicular crags at once began to climb;
And at the top, among the rocks, all seated in a nook,
They saw that Sage a-reading of a most enormous book.

"You earnest Sage!" aloud they cried, "your book you've
read enough in!
We wish to chop you into bits to mix you into Stuffin' ! "

But that old Sage looked calmly up, and with his awful book,
At those two Bachelors' bald heads a certain aim he took;
And over Crag and precipice they rolled promiscuous down,—
At once they rolled, and never stopped in lane or field or town;
And when they reached their house, they found (besides their
want of Stuffin'),
The Mouse had fled—and, previously, had eaten up the Muf-
fin.

They left their home in silence by the once convivial door;
And from that hour those Bachelors were never heard of
more.

THE PELICANS.

THE PELICAN CHORUS

KING and Queen of the Pelicans we;
    No other Birds so grand we see!
None but we have feet like fins!
With lovely leathery throats and chins!
    Ploffskin, Pluffskin, Pelican jee!
    We think no Birds so happy as we!
    Plumpskin, Ploshkin, Pelican jill!
    We think so then, and we thought so still!

We live on the Nile.   The Nile we love.
By night we sleep on the cliffs above;
By day we fish, and at eve we stand
On long bare islands of yellow sand.
And when the sun sinks slowly down,
And the great rock walls grow dark and brown,
Where the purple river rolls fast and dim
And the Ivory Ibis starlike skim,
Wing to wing we dance around,
Stamping our feet with a flumpy sound,

Opening our mouths as Pelicans ought;
And this is the song we nightly snort,—
>> Ploffskin, Pluffskin, Pelican jee!
>> We think no Birds so happy as we!
>> Plumpskin, Ploshkin, Pelican jill!
>> We think so then, and we thought so still!

Last year came out our Daughter Dell,
And all the Birds received her well.
To do her honour a feast we made
For every bird that can swim or wade,—
Herons and Gulls, and Cormorants black,
Cranes, and Flamingoes with scarlet back,
Plovers and Storks, and Geese in clouds,
Swans and Dilberry Ducks in crowds:
Thousands of Birds in wondrous flight!
They ate and drank and danced all night,
And echoing back from the rocks you heard
Multitude-echoes from Bird and Bird,—
>> Ploffskin, Pluffskin, Pelican jee!
>> We think no Birds so happy as we!
>> Plumpskin, Ploshkin, Pelican jill!
>> We think so then, and we thought so still!

Yes, they came; and among the rest
The King of the Cranes all grandly dressed.
Such a lovely tail! Its feathers float
Between the ends of his blue dress-coat;
With pea-green trowsers all so neat,
And a delicate frill to hide his feet
(For though no speaks of it, every one knows
He has got no webs between his toes).
As soon as he saw our Daughter Dell,
In violent love that Crane King fell,—

On seeing her waddling form so fair,
With a wreath of shrimps in her short white hair.
And before the end of the next long day
Our Dell had given her heart away;
For the King of the Cranes had won that heart
With a Crocodile's egg and a large fish-tart.
She vowed to marry the King of the Cranes,
Leaving the Nile for stranger plains;
And away they flew in a gathering crowd
Of endless birds in a lengthening cloud.

       Ploffskin, Pluffskin, Pelican jee!
       We think no Birds so happy as we!
       Plumpskin, Ploshkin, Pelican jill!
       We think so then, and we thought so still!

And far away in the twilight sky
We heard them singing a lessening cry,—
Farther and farther, till out of sight,
And we stood alone in the silent night!
Often since, in the nights of June,
We sit on the sand and watch the moon,—
She has gone to the Great Gromboolian Plain,
And we probably never shall meet again!
Oft, in the long still nights of June,
We sit on the rocks and watch the moon,—
She dwells by the streams of the Chankly Bore.
And we probably never shall see her more.

       Ploffskin, Pluffskin, Pelican jee!
       We think no Birds so happy as we!
       Plumpskin, Ploshkin, Pelican jill!
       We think so then, and we thought so still!

NOTE.—The Air of this and the following song by Edward Lear;
the Arrangement for the Piano by Professor Pomè, of San Remo,
Italy.

THE YONGHY BONGHY BO.

THE COURTSHIP OF THE YONGHY-
BONGHY-BÒ

I

ON the Coast of Coromandel
  Where the early pumpkins blow,
    In the middle of the woods
Lived the Yonghy-Bonghy-Bò.
Two old chairs, and half a candle,
One old jug without a handle,—
    These were all his worldly goods,
    In the middle of the woods,
    These were all his worldly goods,
Of the Yonghy-Bonghy-Bò,
Of the Yonghy-Bonghy Bò.

II

Once, among the Bong-trees walking
  Where the early pumpkins blow,
    To a little heap of stones
Came the Yonghy-Bonghy-Bò.

There he heard a Lady talking,
To some milk-white Hens of Dorking,—
    "'T is the Lady Jingly Jones!
    On that little heap of stones
    Sits the lady Jingly Jones!"
Said the Yonghy-Bonghy-Bò,
Said the Yonghy-Bonghy-Bò.

III

"Lady Jingly! Lady Jingly!
    Sitting where the pumpkins blow,
Will you come and be my wife?"
Said the Yonghy-Bonghy-Bò.
"I am tired of living singly,—
On this coast so wild and shingly,—
    I'm a-weary of my life;
    If you'll come and be my wife,
    Quite serene would be my life!"
Said the Yonghy-Bonghy-Bò,
Said the Yonghy-Bonghy-Bò.

IV

" On this Coast of Coromandel
    Shrimps and watercresses grow,
    Prawns are plentiful and cheap,"
Said the Yonghy-Bonghy-Bò.
" You shall have my chairs and candle,
And my jug without a handle!
    Gaze upon the rolling deep
    (Fish is plentiful and cheap);
    As the sea, my love is deep!"
Said the Yonghy-Bonghy-Bò,
Said the Yonghy-Bonghy-Bò.

V

Lady Jingly answered sadly,
And her tears began to flow,—
"Your proposal comes too late,
Mr. Yonghy-Bonghy-Bò!
I would be your wife most gladly!"
(Here she twirled her fingers madly,)
"But in England I've a mate!
Yes! you've asked me far too late,
For in England I've a mate,
Mr. Yonghy-Bonghy-Bò!
Mr. Yonghy-Bonghy-Bò!

VI

"Mr. Jones (his name is Handel,—
Handel Jones, Esquire, & Co.)
Dorking fowls delights to send,
Mr. Yonghy-Bonghy-Bò!
Keep, oh, keep your chairs and candle,
And your jug without a handle,—
I can merely be your friend!
Should my Jones more Dorkings send,
I will give you three, my friend!
Mr. Yonghy-Bonghy-Bò!
Mr. Yonghy-Bonghy-Bò!

VII

"Though you've such a tiny body,
And your head so large doth grow,—
Though your hat may blow away,
Mr. Yonghy-Bonghy-Bò!
Though you're such a Hoddy Doddy,

[376]

Yet I wish that I could modi-
    fy the words I needs must say!
    Will you please to go away
    That is all I have to say,
Mr. Yonghy-Bonghy-Bò!
Mr. Yonghy-Bonghy-Bò!"

VIII

Down the slippery slopes of Myrtle,
    Where the early pumpkins blow,
    To the calm and silent sea
Fled the Yonghy-Bonghy-Bò.
There, beyond the Bay of Gurtle,
Lay a large and lively Turtle.
    "You're the Cove," he said, "for me;
    On your back beyond the sea,
    Turtle, you shall carry me!"
Said the Yonghy-Bonghy-Bò,
Said the Yonghy-Bonghy-Bò.

IX

Through the silent-roaring ocean
    Did the Turtle swiftly go;

Holding fast upon his shell
Rode the Yonghy-Bonghy-Bò.
With a sad primæval motion
Towards the sunset isles of Boshen
　　Still the Turtle bore him well.
　　Holding fast upon his shell,
　　"Lady Jingly Jones, farewell!"
Sang the Yonghy-Bonghy-Bò.
Sang the Yonghy-Bonghy-Bò.

x

From the Coast of Coromandel
　Did that Lady never go;
　　On that heap of stones she mourns
　For the Yonghy-Bonghy-Bò.
On that Coast of Coromandel,
In his jug without a handle
　　Still she weeps, and daily moans;
　　On that little heap of stones
　　To her Dorking Hens she moans,
　For the Yonghy-Bonghy-Bò,
　For the Yonghy-Bonghy-Bò.

THE POBBLE WHO HAS NO TOES

I

THE Pobble who has no toes
    Had once as many as we;
When they said, " Some day you may lose them all;"
    He replied, " Fish fiddle de-dee! "
And his Aunt Jobiska made him drink
Lavender water tinged with pink;
For she said, " The World in general knows
There's nothing so good for a Pobble's toes! "

II

The Pobble who has no toes,
    Swam across the Bristol Channel;
But before he set out he wrapped his nose
    In a piece of scarlet flannel.
For his Aunt Jobiska said, " No harm
Can come to his toes if his nose is warm;
And it's perfectly known that a Pobble's toes
Are safe—provided he minds his nose."

III

The Pobble swam fast and well,
    And when boats or ships came near him,

He tinkledy-binkledy-winkled a bell
  So that all the world could hear him.
And all the Sailors and Admirals cried,
When they saw him nearing the further side,—
" He has gone to fish, for his Aunt Jobiska's
Runcible Cat with crimson whiskers! "

IV

But before he touched the shore,—
  The shore of the Bristol Channel,
A sea-green Porpoise carried away
  His wrapper of scarlet flannel.
And when he came to observe his feet,
Formerly garnished with toes so neat,
His face at once became forlorn
On perceiving that all his toes were gone!

V

And nobody ever knew,
  From that dark day to the present,
Whoso had taken the Pobble's toes,
  In a manner so far from pleasant.
Whether the shrimps or crawfish grey,
Or crafty Mermaids stole them away,
Nobody knew; and nobody knows
How the Pobble was robbed of his twice five toes!

VI

The Pobble who has no toes
  Was placed in a friendly Bark,
And they rowed him back, and carried him up
  To his Aunt Jobiska's Park.
And she made him a feast, at his earnest wish,
Of eggs and buttercups fried with fish;
And she said, " It's a fact the whole world knows,
That Pobbles are happier without their toes."

[380]

THE NEW VESTMENTS

THERE lived an old man in the Kingdom of Tess,
Who invented a purely original dress;
And when it was perfectly made and complete,
He opened the door and walked into the street.

By way of a hat he'd a loaf of Brown Bread,
In the middle of which he inserted his head;
His Shirt was made up of no end of dead Mice,
The warmth of whose skins was quite fluffy and nice;
His Drawers were of Rabbit-skins, so were his Shoes;
His Stockings were skins, but it is not known whose;
His Waistcoat and Trowsers were made of Pork Chops;
His Buttons were Jujubes and Chocolate Drops;
His Coat was all Pancakes, with Jam for a border,
And a girdle of Biscuits to keep it in order;
And he wore over all, as a screen from bad weather,
A Cloak of green Cabbage-leaves stitched all together.

He had walked a short way, when he heard a great noise,
Of all sorts of Beasticles, Birdlings, and Boys;
And from every long street and dark lane in the town
Beasts, Birdles, and Boys in a tumult rushed down.
Two Cows and a Calf ate his Cabbage-leaf Cloak;
Four Apes seized his Girdle, which vanished like smoke;
Three Kids ate up half of his Pancaky Coat,
And the tails were devour'd by an ancient He Goat;
An army of Dogs in a twinkling tore *up* his
Pork Waistcoat and Trowsers to give to their Puppies;

And while they were growling, and mumbling the Chops,
Ten Boys prigged the Jujubes and Chocolate Drops.
He tried to run back to his house, but in vain,
For scores of fat Pigs came again and again:
They rushed out of stables and hovels and doors;
They tore off his stockings, his shoes, and his drawers;
And now from the housetops with screechings descend
Striped, spotted, white, black, and grey Cats without end:
They jumped on his shoulders and knocked off his hat,
When Crows, Ducks, and Hens made a mincemeat of that;
They speedily flew at his sleeves in a trice,
And utterly tore up his Shirt of dead Mice;
They swallowed the last of his Shirt with a squall,—
Whereon he ran home with no clothes on at all.

And he said to himself, as he bolted the door,
" I will not wear a similar dress any more,
Any more, any more, any more, never more!"

MR. AND MRS. DISCOBBOLOS

I

MR. AND MRS. DISCOBBOLOS
    Climbed to the top of a wall.
And they sate to watch the sunset sky,
And to hear the Nupiter Piffkin cry,
    And the Biscuit Buffalo call.
They took up a roll and some Camomile tea,
And both were as happy as happy could be,
        Till Mrs. Discobbolos said,—
        "Oh! W! X! Y! Z!
        It has just come into my head,
Suppose we should happen to fall! ! ! ! !
        Darling Mr. Discobbolos!

II

" Suppose we should fall down flumpetty,
    Just like pieces of stone,
  On to the thorns, or into the moat,
  What would become of your new green coat?
    And might you not break a bone?
It never occurred to me before,
That perhaps we shall never go down any more!"
        And Mrs. Discobbolos said,
        "Oh! W! X! Y! Z!
        What put it into your head
    To climb up this wall, my own
        Darling Mr. Discobbolos?"
        [383]

III

Mr. Discobbolos answered,
   "At first it gave me pain,
  And I felt my ears turn perfectly pink
  When your exclamation made me think
   We might never get down again!
But now I believe it is wiser far
To remain for ever just where we are."
     And Mr. Discobbolos said,
    "Oh! W! X! Y! Z!
   It has just come into my head
  We shall never go down again,
       Dearest Mrs. Discobbolos!"

IV

So Mr. and Mrs. Discobbolos
   Stood up and began to sing,—
 "Far away from hurry and strife
  Here we will pass the rest of life,
   Ding a dong, ding dong, ding!
We want no knives nor forks nor chairs,
No tables nor carpets nor household cares;
     From worry of life we've fled;
    Oh! W! X! Y! Z!
   There is no more trouble ahead,
 Sorrow or any such thing,
     For Mr. and Mrs. Discobbolos!"

MR. AND MRS. DISCOBBOLOS

I

MR. and Mrs. Discobbolos
  Lived on the top of the wall,
For twenty years, a month and a day,
Till their hair had grown all pearly grey,
  And their teeth began to fall.
They never were ill, or at all dejected,
By all admired, and by some respected,
  Till Mrs. Discobbolos said,
  "O, W! X! Y! Z!
  It has just come into my head,
We have no more room at all —
    Darling Mr. Discobbolos!

II

"Look at our six fine boys!
  And our six sweet girls so fair!
Upon this wall they have all been born,
And not one of the twelve has happened to fall
  Through my maternal care!
Surely they should not pass their lives
Without any chance of husbands or wives!"
  And Mrs. Discobbolos said,
  "O, W! X! Y! Z!
  Did it never come into your head
That our lives must be lived elsewhere,
    Dearest Mr. Discobbolos?
     [385]

III

" They have never been at a ball,
    Nor have even seen a bazaar!
    Nor have heard folks say in a tone all hearty,
    ' What loves of girls (at a garden party)
        Those Misses Discobbolos are!'
Morning and night it drives me wild
To think of the fate of each darling child!"
        But Mr. Discobbolos said,
        "O, W! X! Y! Z!
        What has come into your fiddledum head!
What a runcible goose you are!
        Octopod Mrs. Discobbolos!"

IV

Suddenly Mr. Discobbolos
    Slid from the top of the wall;
    And beneath it he dug a dreadful trench,
    And filled it with dynamite, gunpowder gench,
        And aloud he began to call —
" Let the wild bee sing,
And the blue bird hum!
For the end of your lives has certainly come!"
        And Mrs. Discobbolos said,
        "O, W! X! Y! Z!
        We shall presently all be dead,
On this ancient runcible wall,
            Terrible Mr. Discobbolos!"

V

Pensively, Mr. Discobbolos
    Sat with his back to the wall;
    He lighted a match, and fired the train,

[886]

And the mortified mountain echoed again
  To the sound of an awful fall!
And all the Discobbolos family flew
In thousands of bits to the sky so blue,
  And no one was left to have said,
  "O, W! X! Y! Z!
  Has it come into anyone's head
That the end has happened to all
   Of the whole of the Clan Discobbolos?"

.

THE QUANGLE WANGLE'S HAT

I

ON the top of the Crumpetty Tree
  The Quangle Wangle sat,
But his face you could not see,
  On account of his Beaver Hat.
For his Hat was a hundred and two feet wide,
With ribbons and bibbons on every side,
And bells, and buttons, and loops, and lace,
So that nobody ever could see the face
  Of the Quangle Wangle Quee.

II

The Quangle Wangle said
  To himself on the Crumpetty Tree,
  "Jam, and jelly, and bread
  Are the best of food for me!
But the longer I live on this Crumpetty Tree
The plainer than ever it seems to me
That very few people come this way
And that life on the whole is far from gay!"
  Said the Quangle Wangle Quee.

III

But there came to the Crumpetty Tree
  Mr. and Mrs. Canary;
And they said, " Did ever you see
  Any spot so charmingly airy?
May we build a nest on your lovely Hat?
Mr. Quangle Wangle, grant us that!
O please let us come and build a nest
Of whatever material suits you best,
     Mr. Quangle Wangle Quee!"

IV

And besides, to the Crumpetty Tree
  Came the Stork, the Duck, and the Owl;
The Snail and the Bumble-Bee,
  The Frog and the Fimble Fowl
'(The Fimble Fowl, with a Corkscrew leg);
And all of them said, " We humbly beg
We may build our homes on your lovely Hat,—
Mr. Quangle Wangle, grant us that!
     Mr. Quangle Wangle Quee!"

V

And the Golden Grouse came there,
  And the Pobble who has no toes,
And the small Olympian bear,
  And the Dong with a luminous nose.
And the Blue Baboon who played the flute,
And the Orient Calf from the Land of Tute,
And the Attery Squash, and the Bisky Bat,—
All came and built on the lovely Hat
    Of the Quangle Wangle Quee.

VI

'And the Quangle Wangle said
  To himself on the Crumpetty Tree,
"When all these creatures move
   What a wonderful noise there'll be!"
And at night by the light of the Mulberry moon
They danced to the Flute of the Blue Baboon,
On the broad green leaves of the Crumpetty Tree,
And all were as happy as happy could be,
     With the Quangle Wangle Quee.

THE CUMMERBUND

AN INDIAN POEM

I

SHE sate upon her Dobie,
  To watch the Evening Star,
And all the Punkahs, as they passed,
  Cried, " My! how fair you are! "
Around her bower, with quivering leaves,
  The tall Kamsamahs grew,
And Kitmutgars in wild festoons
  Hung down from Tchokis blue.

II

Below her home the river rolled
  With soft meloobious sound,
Where golden-finned Chuprassies swam,
  In myriads circling round.
Above, on tallest trees remote
  Green Ayahs perched alone,
And all night long the Mussak moan'd
  Its melancholy tone.

III

And where the purple Nullahs threw
  Their branches far and wide,
And silvery Goreewallahs flew
  In silence, side by side,

The little Bheesties' twittering cry
   Rose on the flagrant air,
'And oft the angry Jampan howled
   Deep in his hateful lair.

IV

She sate upon her Dobie,
   She heard the Nimmak hum,
When all at once a cry arose,
   " The Cummerbund is come! "
In vain she fled: with open jaws
   The angry monster followed,
And so (before assistance came)
   That Lady Fair was swollowed.

V

They sought in vain for even a bone
   Respectfully to bury;
They said, " Hers was a dreadful fate! "
   (And Echo answered, " Very.")
They nailed her Dobie to the wall,
   Where last her form was seen,
And underneath they wrote these words,
   In yellow, blue, and green:

" Beware, ye Fair! Ye Fair, beware!
   Nor sit out late at night,
Lest horrid Cummerbunds should come,
   And swollow you outright."

Note.—First published in *Times of India*, Bombay, July, 1874.

THE AKOND OF SWAT.

WHO, or why, or which, or *what,*   Is the Akond of SWAT?

Is he tall or short, or dark or fair?
Does he sit on a stool or a sofa or chair,
                                    or SQUAT?
                              The Akond of Swat?

Is he wise or foolish, young or old?
Does he drink his soup and his coffee cold,
                                    or HOT,
                              The Akond of Swat?

Does he sing or whistle, jabber or talk,
And when riding abroad does he gallop or walk,
                                    or TROT,
                              The Akond of Swat?

Does he wear a turban, a fez, or a hat?
Does he sleep on a mattress, a bed, or a mat,
                                    or a COT,
                              The Akond of Swat?

When he writes a copy in round-hand size,
Does he cross his T's and finish his I's
                                    with a DOT,
                              The Akond of Swat?

Can he write a letter concisely clear
Without a speck or a smudge or smear
                                    or BLOT,
                              The Akond of Swat?

Do his people like him extremely well?
Or do they, whenever they can, rebel,
                                    or PLOT,
                              At the Akind of Swat?

If he catches them then, either old or young,
Does he have them chopped in pieces or hung,
                                    or *shot,*
                              The Akond of Swat?

Do his people prig in the lanes or park?
Or even at times, when days are dark,
                                    GAROTTE?
                              O the Akond of Swat!

Does he study the wants of his own dominion?
Or doesn't he care for public opinion
                                    a JOT,
                              The Akond of Swat?

[393]

To amuse his mind do his people show him
Pictures, or any one's last new poem,   or WHAT,
                                                  For the Akond of Swat?

At night if he suddenly screams and wakes,
Do they bring him only a few small cakes,   or a LOT,
                                                  For the Akond of Swat?

Does he live on turnips, tea, or tripe?
Does he like his shawl to be marked with a stripe,   or a DOT,
                                                  The Akond of Swat?

Does he like to lie on his back in a boat
Like the lady who lived in that isle remote,   SHALLOTT,
                                                  The Akond of Swat?

Is he quiet, or always making a fuss?
Is his steward a Swiss or a Swede or a Russ,   or a SCOT,
                                                  The Akond of Swat?

Does he like to sit by the calm blue wave?
Or to sleep and snore in a dark green cave,   or a GROTT,
                                                  The Akond of Swat?

Does he drink small beer from a silver jug?
Or a bowl? or a glass? or a cup? or a mug?   or a POT,
                                                  The Akond of Swat?

Does he beat his wife with a gold-topped pipe,
When she lets the gooseberries grow too ripe,   or ROT,
                                                  The Akond of Swat?

Does he wear a white tie when he dines with friends,
And tie it neat in a bow with ends,   or a KNOT,
                                                  The Akond of Swat?

Does he like new cream, and hate mince-pies?
When he looks at the sun does he wink his eyes,   or NOT,
                                                  The Akond of Swat?

Does he teach his subjects to roast and bake?
Does he sail about on an inland lake,   in a YACHT,
                                                  The Akond of Swat?

Some one, or nobody, knows I wot
Who or which or why or what   Is the Akond of Swat!

NOTE.—For the existence of this potentate see Indian newspapers, *passim*. The proper way to read the verses is to make an immense emphasis on the monosyllabic rhymes, which indeed ought to be shouted out by a chorus.

INCIDENTS IN THE LIFE OF MY UNCLE ARLY

I

O MY agèd Uncle Arly!
　　Sitting on a heap of Barley
　　　　Thro' the silent hours of night,—
Close beside a leafy thicket:—
On his nose there was a Cricket,—
In his hat a Railway-Ticket;—
　　　　(But his shoes were far too tight.)

II

Long ago, in youth, he squander'd
All his goods away, and wander'd
　　　　To the Tiniskoop-hills afar.
There on golden sunsets blazing,
Every evening found him gazing,—
Singing,—" Orb! you're quite amazing!
　　　　" How I wonder what you are!"

III

Like the ancient Medes and Persians,
Always by his own exertions
　　　　He subsisted on those hills; —
Whiles,—by teaching children spelling,—
Or at times by merely yelling,—
Or at intervals by selling
　　　　" Propter's Nicodemus Pills."

IV

Later, in his morning rambles
He perceived the moving brambles—
     Something square and white disclose;—
'Twas a First-class Railway Ticket;
But, on stooping down to pick it
Off the ground,—a pea-green Cricket
     Settled on my uncle's Nose.

V

Never—never more,—oh! never,
Did that Cricket leave him ever,—
     Dawn or evening, day or night;—
Clinging as a constant treasure,—
Chirping with a cheerious measure,—
Wholly to my uncle's pleasure,—
     (Though his shoes were far too tight.)

VI

So for three-and-forty winters,
Till his shoes were worn to splinters,
     All those hills he wander'd o'er,—
Sometimes silent;—sometimes yelling;—
Till he came to Borley-Melling,
Near his old ancestral dwelling;—
     (But his shoes were far too tight.)

VII

On a little heap of Barley
Died my agèd uncle Arly,
     And they buried him one night;—
Close beside the leafy thicket;—
There,—his hat and Railway-Ticket;—
There,—his ever-faithful Cricket;—
     (But his shoes were far too tight.)

ECLOGUE

COMPOSED AT CANNES, DECEMBER 9TH, 1867

(Interlocutors—Mr. Lear and Mr. and Mrs. Symonds.)

Edwardus.—What makes you look so black, so glum, so cross?
    Is it neuralgia, headache, or remorse?

Johannes.—What makes you look as cross, or even more so?
    Less like a man than is a broken Torso?

E.—What if my life is odious, should I grin?
    If you are savage, need I care a pin?

J.—And if I suffer, am I then an owl?
    May I not frown and grind my teeth and growl?

E.—Of course you may; but may not I growl too?
    May I not frown and grind my teeth like you?

J.—See Catherine comes!   To her, to her,
    Let each his several miseries refer;
    She shall decide whose woes are least or worst,
    And which, as growler, shall rank last or first.

Catherine.—Proceed to growl, in silence I'll attend,
    And hear your foolish growlings to the end;

[397]

And when they're done, I shall correctly judge
Which of your griefs are real or only fudge.
Begin, let each his mournful voice prepare,
(And pray, however angry, do not swear!)

J.—We came abroad for warmth, and find sharp cold!
Cannes is an imposition, and we're sold.

E.—Why did I leave my native land, to find
Sharp hailstones, snow, and most disgusting
wind?

J.—What boots it that we orange trees or lemons see,
If we must suffer from *such* vile inclemency?

E.—Why did I take the lodgings I have got,
Where all I don't want is:—all I want not!

J.—Last week I called aloud, O! O! O! O!
The ground is wholly overspread with snow!
Is that at any rate a theme for mirth
Which makes a sugar-cake of all the earth?

E.—Why must I sneeze and snuffle, groan and cough,
If my hat's on my head, or if it's off?
Why must I sink all poetry in this prose,
The everlasting blowing of my nose?

J.—When I walk out the mud my footsteps clogs,
Besides, I suffer from attacks of dogs.

E.—Me a vast awful bulldog, black and brown,
Completely terrified when near the town;

[898]

As calves, perceiving butchers, trembling reel,
So did *my* calves the approaching monster feel.

J.—Already from two rooms we're driven away,
Because the beastly chimneys smoke all day:
Is this a trifle, say? Is this a joke?
That we, like hams, should be becooked in smoke?

E.—Say, what avails it that my servant speaks
Italian, English, Arabic, and Greek,
Besides Albanian: if he don't speak French,
How can he ask for salt, or shrimps, or tench?

J.—When on the foolish hearth fresh wood I place,
It whistles, sings, and squeaks, before my face:
And if it does unless the fire burns bright,
And if it does, yet squeaks, how can I write?

E.—Alas! I needs must go and call on swells,
That they may say, " Pray draw me the Es-
trelles."
On one I went last week to leave a card,
The swell was out—the servant eyed me hard:
" This chap's a thief disguised," his face ex-
pressed:
If I go there again, may I be blest!

J.—Why must I suffer in this wind and gloom?
Roomattics in a vile cold attic room?

E.—Swells drive about the road with haste and fury,
As Jehu drove about all over Jewry.

[399]

Just now, while walking slowly, I was all but
Run over by the Lady Emma Talbot,
Whom not long since a lovely babe I knew,
With eyes and cap-ribbons of perfect blue.

J.—Downstairs and upstairs, every blessed minute,
There's each room with pianofortes in it.
How can I write with noises such as those?
And, being always discomposed, compose?

E.—Seven Germans through my garden lately
strayed,
And all on instruments of torture played:
They blew, they screamed, they yelled: how can
I paint
Unless my room is quiet, which it ain't?

J.—How can I study if a hundred flies
Each moment blunder into both my eyes?

E.—How can I draw with green or blue or red,
If flies and beetles vex my old bald head?

J.—How can I translate German Metaphys-
-Ics, if mosquitoes round my forehead whizz?

E.—I've bought some bacon (though it's much too
fat),
But round the house there prowls a hideous cat:
Once should I see my bacon in her mouth,
What care I if my rooms look north or south?

J.—Pain from a pane in one cracked window comes,
    Which sings and whistles, buzzes, shrieks and
        hums;
    In vain amain with pain the pane with this chord
    I fain would strain to stop the beastly *dis*cord!

E.—If rain and wind and snow and such like ills
    Continue here, how shall I pay my bills?
    For who through cold and slush and rain will
        come
    To see my drawings and to purchase some?
    And if they don't, what destiny is mine?
    How can I ever get to Palestine?

J.—The blinding sun strikes through the olive trees,
    When I walk out, and always makes me sneeze.

E.—Next door, if all night long the moon is shining,
    There sits a dog, who wakes me up with whining.

Cath.—Forbear! You both are bores, you've growled
        enough:
    No longer will I listen to such stuff!
    All men have nuisances and bores to afflict 'um:
    Hark then, and bow to my official dictum!
    For you, Johannes, there is most excuse,
    (Some interruptions are the very deuce),
    You're younger than the other cove, who surely
    Might have some sense—besides, you're some-
        what poorly.
    This therefore is my sentence, that you nurse
    The Baby for seven hours, and nothing worse.

[401]

For you, Edwardus, I shall say no more
Than that your griefs are fudge, yourself a bore:
Return at once to cold, stewed, minced, hashed
    mutton—
To wristbands ever guiltless of a button—
To raging winds and sea (where don't you wish
Your luck may ever let you catch one fish?)—

To make large drawings nobody will buy—
To paint oil pictures which will never dry—
To write new books which nobody will read—
To drink weak tea, on tough old pigs to feed—
Till spring-time brings the birds and leaves and
    flowers,
And time restores a world of happier hours.

NONSENSE ALPHABETS

A

A was an Area Arch
    Where washerwomen sat;
They made a lot of lovely starch
    To starch Papa's Cravat.

B

B was a Bottle blue,
    Which was not very small;
Papa he filled it full of beer,
    And then he drank it all.

[405]

C

C was Papa's grey Cat,
  Who caught a squeaky Mouse;
She pulled him by his twirly tail
  All about the house.

D

D was Papa's white Duck,
  Who had a curly tail;
One day it ate a great fat frog,
  Besides a leetle snail.

E

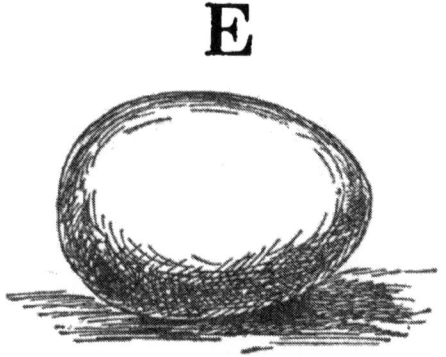

E was a little Egg,
 Upon the breakfast table;
Papa came in and ate it up
 As fast as he was able.

F

F was a little Fish.
 Cook in the river took it.
Papa said, " Cook! Cook! bring a dish!
 And, Cook! be quick and cook it!"

G

G was Papa's new Gun;
  He put it in a box;
And then he went and bought a bun,
And walked about the Docks.

H

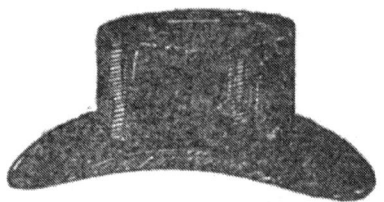

H was Papa's new Hat;
  He wore it on his head;
Outside it was completely black,
  But inside it was red.

I

I was an Inkstand new,
    Papa he likes to use it;
He keeps it in his pocket now,
    For fear that he should lose it.

J

J was some Apple Jam,
    Of which Papa ate part;
But all the rest he took away
    And stuffed into a tart.

[409]

K

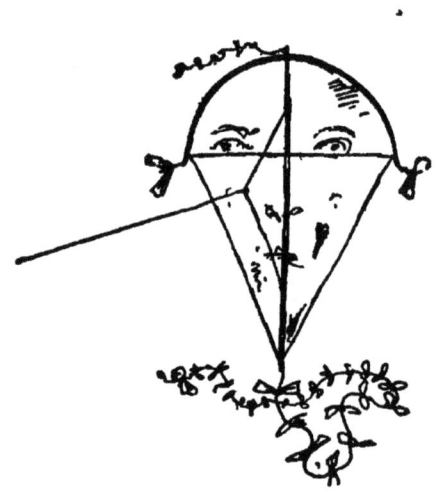

K was a great new Kite;
Papa he saw it fly
Above a thousand chimney pots,
And all about the sky.

L

L was a fine new Lamp;
But when the wick was lit,
Papa he said, " This Light ain't good!
I cannot read a bit ! "

M

M was a dish of mince;
It looked so good to eat!
Papa, he quickly ate it up,
And said, " This is a treat! "

[411]

N

N was a Nut that grew
    High up upon a tree;
  Papa, who could not reach it, said,
    " That's *much* too high for me!"

O was an Owl who flew
    All in the dark away,
  Papa said, "What an owl you are!
    Why don't you fly by day?"

P

P was a little Pig,
 Went out to take a walk;
Papa he said, " If Piggy dead,
 He'd all turn into Pork! "

Q

Q was a Quince that hung
 Upon a garden tree;
Papa he brought it with him home,
 And ate it with his tea.

R

R was a Railway Rug
Extremely large and warm;
Papa he wrapped it round his head,
In a most dreadful storm.

S

S was Papa's new Stick,
Papa's new thumping Stick,
To thump extremely wicked boys,
Because it was so thick.

T

T was a tumbler full
 Of Punch all hot and good;
Papa he drank it up, when in
 The middle of a wood.

U

U was a silver urn,
 Full of hot scalding water;
Papa said, " If that Urn were mine,
 I'd give it to my daughter!"

V

V was a Villain; once
    He stole a piece of beef.
Papa ne said, " Oh, dreadful man!
    That Villain is a Thief!"

W

W was a Watch of Gold:
    It told the time of day,
So that Papa knew when to come,
    And when to go away.

X

X was King Xerxes, whom
    Papa much wished to know;
But this he could not do, because
    Xerxes died long ago.

Y

Y was a Youth, who kicked
    And screamed and cried like mad;
Papa he said, " Your conduct is
    Abominably bad! "

Z

Z was a Zebra striped
  And streaked with lines of black;
Papa said once, he thought he'd like
  A ride upon his back.

ALPHABET

A   tumbled down, and hurt his Arm, against a bit of wood.

B   said, "My Boy, oh, do not cry; it cannot do you good!"

C   said, "A Cup of Coffee hot can't do you any harm."

D   said, "A Doctor should be fetched, and he would cure the arm."

E   said, "An Egg beat up with milk would quickly make him well."

F   said, "A Fish, if broiled, might cure, if only by the smell."

G   said, "Green Gooseberry fool, the best of cures I hold."

H   said, "His Hat should be kept on, to keep him from the cold."

I   said, "Some Ice upon his head will make him better soon."

J   said, "Some Jam, if spread on bread, or given in a spoon!"

L   said, "A Kangaroo is here,—this picture let him see."

K   said, "A Lamp pray keep alight, to make some barley tea."

M   said, "A Mulberry or two might give him satisfaction."

N   said, "Some Nuts, if rolled about, might be a slight attraction."

O   said, "An Owl might make him laugh, if only it would wink."

P   said, "Some Poetry might be read aloud, to make him think."

Q   said, "A Quince I recommend,—a Quince, or else a Quail."

R   said, "Some Rats might make him move, if fastened by their tail."

S   said, "A Song should now be sung, in hopes to make him laugh!"

T   said, "A Turnip might avail, if sliced or cut in half!"

U   said, "An Urn, with water hot, place underneath his chin!"

V   said, "I'll stand upon a chair, and play a Violin!"

W   said, "Some Whisky-Whizzgigs fetch, some marbles and a ball!"

X   said, "Some double XX ale would be the best of all!"

Y   said, "Some Yeast mixed up with salt would make a perfect plaster!"

Z   said, "Here is a box of Zinc! Get in, my little master!
We'll shut you up! We'll nail you down! We will, my little master!
We think we've all heard quite enough of this your sad disaster!"

HOW PLEASANT TO KNOW MR. LEAR

THE following lines by Mr. Lear were written for a young lady of his acquaintance, who had quoted to him the words of a young lady not of his acquaintance, "How Pleasant to know Mr. Lear!"

"How pleasant to know Mr. Lear!"
　　Who has written such volumes of stuff!
Some think him ill-tempered and queer,
　　But a few think him pleasant enough.

His mind is concrete and fastidious,
　　His nose is remarkably big;
His visage is more or less hideous,
　　His beard it resembles a wig.

He has ears, and two eyes, and ten fingers,
　　Leastways if you reckon two thumbs;
Long ago he was one of the singers,
　　But now he is one of the dumbs.

He sits in a beautiful parlour,
　　With hundreds of books on the wall;
He drinks a great deal of Marsala,
　　But never gets tipsy at all.

He has many friends, lay men and clerical,
　　Old Foss is the name of his cat;
His body is perfectly spherical,
　　He weareth a runcible hat.

When he walks in waterproof white,
  The children run after him so!
Calling out, " He's come out in his night-
  Gown, that crazy old Englishman, oh!"

He weeps by the side of the ocean,
  He weeps on the top of the hill;
He purchases pancakes and lotion,
  And chocolate shrimps from the mill.

He reads, but he cannot speak, Spanish,
  He cannot abide ginger beer:
Ere the days of his pilgrimage vanish,
  How pleasant to know Mr. Lear!

FROM THE LETTERS

FROM THE LETTERS

O! MIMBER FOR THE COUNTY LOUTH

O MIMBER for the County Louth
    Residing at Ardee!
Whom, I, before I wander South
    Partik'lar wish to see:—

I send you this.—That you may know
    I've left the Sussex shore,
And coming here two days ago
    Do cough for evermore.

Or gasping hard for breath do sit
    Upon a brutal chair,
For to lie down in Asthma fit
    Is what I cannot bear.

Or sometimes sneeze: and always blow
    My well-developed nose.
And altogether never know
    No comfort nor repose.

All through next week I shall be here,
    To work as best I may,
On my last picture, which is near-
    -er finished every day.

THERE WAS AN OLD MAN WHO FELT PERT

THERE was an old man who felt pert
    When he wore a pale rose-coloured shirt.
When they said " Is it pleasant? "
He cried " Not at present—
It's a *leetle* too short—is my shirt! "

BUT AH! (THE LANDSCAPE PAINTER SAID)

BUT ah! (the Landscape painter said,)
    A brutal fly walks on my head
And my bald skin doth tickle;
And so I stop distracted quite,
(With itching skin for who can write?)
In most disgusting pickle—

THERE WAS AN OLD PERSON OF PAXO

THERE was an old person of Paxo
    Which complained when the fleas bit his back so,
But they gave him a chair
And impelled him to swear,
Which relieved that old person of Paxo.

TENNYSONIAN PARODIES

1. Like the Wag who jumps at evening
   All along the sanded floor.

2. To watch the tipsy cripples on the beach,
   With topsy turvy signs of screamy play.

6. Tom-Morry Pathos;—all things bare,—
      With such a turkey! such a hen!
      And scrambling forms of distant men,
   O!—ain't you glad you were not there!

4. Delirious Bulldogs;—echoing, calls
      My daughter,—green as summer grass:—
      The long supine Plebeian ass,
   The nasty crockery boring falls;—

5. Spoon meat at Bill Porter's in the Hall,
   With green pomegranates, and no end of Bass.

O! CHICHESTER, MY CARLINGFORD!

OH! Chichester, my Carlingford!
    O! Parkinson, my Sam!
O! SPQ, my Fortescue!
   How awful glad I am!

For now you'll do no more hard work
Because by sudden pleasing-jerk
   You're all at once a peer,—
Whereby I cry, God bless the Queen!
As was, and is, and still has been,
   Yours ever, Edward Lear.

SAITH THE POET OF NONSENSE

SAITH the Poet of Nonsense
" Thoughts into my head do come
Thick as flies upon a plum."

WHEN " GRAND OLD MEN " PERSIST IN FOLLY

WHEN " Grand old men " persist in folly
In slaughtering men and chopping trees,
What art can soothe the melancholy
Of those whom futile " statesmen " teaze?

The only way their wrath to cover
To let mankind know who's to blame-o—
Is first to rush by train to Dover
And then straight onward to Sanremo.

IT IS A VIRTUE IN INGENUOUS YOUTH

IT is a virtue in ingenuous youth,
To leave off lying and return to truth,
For well it's known that all religious morals
Are caused by Bass's Ale and South Atlantic Corals.

HIS GARDEN

AND this is certain; if so be
You could just now my garden see,
The aspic of my flowers so bright
Would make you shudder with delight.

And if you voz to see my rozziz
As is a boon to all men's nozziz,—
You'd fall upon your back and scream—
"O Lawk! O criky! it's a dream!"

— E. 13. June 1880.

O Brother Chicken! Sister Chick,
  O gracious me! O my!
This broken Eggshell was anyhome!
    I wish with my egg!
However did I get inside? Or how did I get out
And must my life be evermore, an atmosphere of dou

Can no one tell? Can no one solve, this mystery of Eg
Or why we chirp & flap our wings, — or why we're all 2 le
And since we cannot understand, ——
    May it not seem to me,
That we are merely born by chance,
    Egg-nostics for to be?

                              Edward
                              Wimbledon Comm